Why I Believe These Are the Last Days

Why I Believe These Are the Last Days

Hearthstone
Publishing Ltd.

P.O. Box 815·Oklahoma City, Ok 73101

A Division Of
Southwest Radio Church Of The Air

All scripture references are from the King James Version unless otherwise stated.

Why I Believe These Are the Last Days
Revised Edition, 1990
Copyright © by **Hearthstone Publishing**
Oklahoma City, OK 73101

Printed in the United States of America

Published by:
Hearthstone Publishing
P.O. Box 1144
Oklahoma City, OK 73101

Library of Congress Catalog Card Number 90-84589
ISBN 0-9624517-7-0

In Recognition

The ministry of The Southwest Radio Church extends special thanks to our Watchmen and other faithful backers and supporters who gave so generously to make possible the publication of this book:

Watchman Honor Roll
Co-Sponsors

A.P. Anderson

Lois C. Calise

Carl Gautreaux

Paul Godin

Mr. and Mrs. John Golden

Avis W. Goorman

Robert Hortin

Mrs. Sophie K. Hukill

Richard Kender

Theodore Ritota, M.D.

J.H. "Rod" Rodda

Charles Rosemond

Roger Starkey

Leo Teneese

Mr. & Mrs. Hamilton Treadway

Roosevelt Turner

Tom Vallejo

Co-Publishers

Leo Affi

Mr. and Mrs. Ron Bashista

Russ Beirele

Anthony Bennett

Dalfina Bennett

Mrs. Thomas W. Bevan

Mr. and Mrs. Ernest Bodine

Edward Bottelman

Mrs. June Boyd

Russell C. Burnham

Evelyn Calley

John Cameron

James and Mary Chorlton

Mrs. Harlan Clark

Duncan and Elizabeth Clyne

Clifford Cochran

Jerry Cochran

Keith Cox

Mrs. Fred Craig

Sam E. Crawford

William Cribb

Ben C. Davis

Mrs. Ann Eshelman

Rachel J. Faber

Barbaralu Fischer

Susan Girouard

Mr. and Mrs. Frank Gregbrin

G.E. Groseclose

Robert L. Gunderson

Willis D. Hanson

Mr. and Mrs. Maurice Harbin

Larry Havlicek

Morris Hill

Mark Hoff, M.D.

Stewart Houston, Jr.

Mrs. Evelyn Jackson

David Kennedy

Edward Koval

Robery Lakey

Lincoln Lakoff

Mrs. E.V. League

Rick and Bonnie Letz

Mrs. Florence Lindsey

F.M. Loftus

Lorna/PSI Communications, Inc.

Lelia Luchen

Mr. and Mrs. George Lyddon

Suzanne Mack

Kevin Markey

Modena Mayfield

Alice L. McDonald

Stephen Mitchell

Larry Orr

Hector Paz

Mrs. John W. Pick

Todd Pierce

G. Pluto

Marianne Prefontaine

Fero P. Rice

Mr. and Mrs. Robert Scott

Will Scott

J. Doris Scofield

Wayne F. Sievert

Mrs. Robert Skold

Diane Stewart

Dale V. Stevenson

Erma Stites

Dr. and Mrs. Joseph Strother

Roland Takami

Leonard Taylor

Mrs. Nathan A. Toalson

Chris Thompson

Sarah Thornbury
Robert Turnipseed
Mrs. Louise Ulander

Alfred Van Eenwyk
Helen Wilkening
Al Wilsinson

About the Authors

Reverend Noah Hutchings, for the past thirty-five years has been active in research and writing for the daily radio programs for *The Southwest Radio Church*. He is recognized for his great knowledge of the Middle East and frequently speaks on prophetic subjects in various meetings throughout the nation. Reverend Hutchings is editor of *The Gospel Truth*, a monthly publication of the radio ministry.

Dr. Carl Baugh is the founder and director of Creation Evidences Museum in Glen Rose, Texas. Dr. Baugh is known internationally and as a minister and special creation speaker. In addition to degrees in theology, he holds a Masters degree in archaeology from Pacific College, and a Doctor of Philosophy degree in anthropology from College of Advanced Education in conjunction with Pacific International University.

Dr. Baugh accepted the premise of evolution while in school, but afterward came to the conclusion that only creation account in the Bible held the answers to life on earth and the laws which govern the universe.

Grant Jeffrey has over twenty-five years of research and teaching experience in the area of Bible prophecy and history. His research in Israel and Europe, plus his teaching at many Bible colleges and churches led him to put forth his fascinating conclusions in his book, *Armageddon — Appointment With Destiny.*

J.R. Church hosts *Prophecy In the News*, a weekly syndicated television program in cities across America. He travels extensively, speaking in prophetic conferences, and publishes a monthly newspaper on prophetic research.

Dr. Rob Lindsted, Ph.D., has taught engineering on the university level for over ten years. He is an engineering consultant, working for over one hundred different companies. As a Bible conference speaker and teacher, he enjoys working with young people. Rob Lindsted speaks over a daily radio program called *Bible Truth*, and appears as a guest speaker on other programs.

Dr. Emil Gaverluk, Ph.D., Ed.D., M.Div., has held pastorates in several large churches. He was a speaker and research writer for *The Southwest Radio Church.* Dr. Gaverluk has traveled abroad and written several books.

Don McAlvany broadcasts the *McAlvany Intelligence Advisor*, a weekly economic, financial, and geopolitical analysis of events happening around the world which affect you, your family, and your finances. He is also the author of the *McAlvany Intelligence Advisor*, a monthly monetary, economic, and geopolitical newsletter designed to help people in general and Christians in particular to understand the critical issues of our day, how these issues can affect them financially, politically, and what to do about these issues.

Dr. Dave Breese, president of Christian Destiny Ministries, is an internationally known author, lecturer, radio and television broadcaster, and Christian minister active in the field of evangelism. A prolific writer, he has written six full-length books, and many booklets and magazine features. He is heard nationally with *Pause For Good News* daily and on *Dave Breese Reports* weekly which concentrates on world events from a biblical point of view. Dr. Breese is also the publisher of *Destiny Newsletter*, which contains incisive comments on the tide of our times from a Christian perspective.

William Sillings, a pastor since 1975, is currently pastor of the Church of the BIble Covenant in Oklahoma City. Her serves as editor for both *Fellowship* magazine and also for Fellowship Publications, the publishing organization of the Fellowship of Bible Churches.

Table Of Contents

Foreward

by N.W. Hutchings

"And if I go and prepare a place for you, I will come again, and receive you unto myself; that where I am, there ye may be also" (John 14:3).

"For as the lightning cometh out of the east, and shineth even unto the west; so shall also the coming of the Son of man be" (Matt. 24:27).

The angelic messengers informed the disciples on the day of Jesus' return to the Father, *". . . this same Jesus, which is taken up from you into heaven, shall so come in like manner as ye have seen him go into heaven"* (Acts 1:11).

In every chapter in Paul's two epistles to the church at Thessalonica, the return of Jesus Christ is declared to be an irrevocable promise of God. Therefore, the question is not *if* He is coming, but rather *when* is He coming?

Now that we have established that Jesus Christ is coming back from Heaven to this earth, can the time of His return be known? This is a debatable question. Jesus said of His coming again in Matthew 24:36: *"But of that day and hour knoweth no man, no, not the angels of heaven, but my Father only."*

Some who have studied the particular wording of the Greek text contend that while no date is published in the Bible for the Lord's return, it can be ascertained by investigation. Edgar Whisenant published a controversial book entitled *88 Reasons Why the Rapture Will Be In 1988*. Jesus did not come in the air in 1988 to translate the church. Mr Whisenant explained that he was off one year in his calculations, so he published a new edition entitled *The Final Shout — Rapture '89 Report*. The new date for the rapture, according to Mr. Whisenant, was September 1, 1989. Once again he was in error.

There are numerical patterns in creation and in God's revelations to the prophets of Israel which indicate the end of the present age by the year 2000 A.D.. However, exact date setting is arrived at by conclusion rather than by stated fact, and although there have been many date-setters for the Lord's return, all to this time have been wrong.

We do not wish to belabor the point of whether it is possible, or not possible, to determine the exact date for the rapture or the return of Jesus Christ to establish His kingdom here on earth. What we can affirm is the certainty of knowing when His coming is near. In fact, God wants His people to know when the time of the end of the age is near. Otherwise, Jesus Christ would not have given a multitude of signs of the last days within the content of the Olivet Discourse.

In 1 Thessalonians 5:1-10, the Apostle Paul stated that the unsaved world will be oblivious to the times of the last days, but that Christians who are discerning the signs of the times can know when the day that destruction will come upon the world is near. Of the nearness of the Lord's return Paul said, *"But of the times and the seasons, brethren, ye have no need that I write unto you"* (1 Thess. 5:1). On the Hebrew calendar, a "time" was a year, and "times" was two or more years, but certainly no more than one generation. Within one year there are four seasons.

Without having to stretch the truth of God's Word, we can securely aver that according to Bible prophecy, Christians who are faithfully and accurately comparing world events to the prophetic Word can know within a few years, or even months, when the events associated with the last seven years of the present dispensation will begin to occur.

In this volume noted scholars of eschatology declare why they believe we are living in the last days which precede the coming of Jesus Christ.

Chapter One

Increase Of Knowledge and Communication

by N.W. Hutchings

The prophet Daniel wrote over twenty-five hundred years ago that at "... *the time of the end: many shall run to and fro, and knowledge shall be increased*" (Dan. 12:4). In reference to the sequence of end-time events, the prophet wrote "... *the end thereof shall be with a flood ...*" (Dan. 9:26).

The prophetic scope of the world economy at the time of Christ's return depicts a sudden rush, like a flood, of political, financial, and scientific changes that will literally shake the earth to prepare the way for that "man of sin," the Antichrist. The Word of God indicates plainly that the generation of mankind living at the end of the age could witness these dramatic events and know by observing these signs that the coming of the Lord from Heaven was at hand, even at the door. We read in Luke 21:28, *"And when these things begin to come to pass, then look up, and lift up your heads; for your redemption draweth nigh."* Further assurance that

4

Christians who are discerning the signs of the times can know when the coming of the Lord is near is clearly stated in 1 Thessalonians 5:4: *"But ye, brethren, are not in darkness, that that day should overtake you as a thief."*

I believe we are living in the last days because of the sudden rush of knowledge, communications, and modern inventions. A seventy-year-old man or woman today has lived on earth approximately one percent off the time from the creation of Adam. Yet, let us consider what has happened in this one-hundredth of the time (according to Ussher's chronology) since man was created.

1. Seventy-five percent of all medicines and drugs in use today have been discovered in our lifetime.
2. Ninety percent of all the scientists who ever lived are alive today.
3. The atom has been split. Nuclear weapons that have been developed as a result are so destructive that one such device exceeds in power all the bombs and artillery shells exploded in World War One and World War Two combined.
4. There has been development of a space exploration program that has sent men to the moon, and space ships to other planets in our solar system.
5. There is exaltation of man's intelligence through an education explosion which boasts the doubling of man's knowledge every two and a half years.
6. There has been the invention and development of radio, television, and other mass communication

systems with capabilities to broadcast news around the world in a matter of seconds.

7. There has been the invention and development of the computer, making possible a cashless economic system whereby all the world may one day be working, buying, and selling with nothing more than code marks and numbers.

Virtually all of the aforementioned scientific developments were unknown at the beginning of the present century. In fact, practically all of the modern conveniences like automobiles, television, telephones, airplanes, and computers were either produced or perfected in my lifetime. I have been privileged to live in that one percent of time that has seen all of these things come to pass. It is no wonder that Bible prophecy has so much to say about the last days, because in so many ways, it is as if six thousand years were compressed into one generation.

As we consider the seven-year tribulation period with armies moving across the face of the earth, with the climax of the ages occurring in a brief span of time, such a flood of end-time prophetic developments could not happen without the increase of knowledge and communication prophesied in the Bible. But let us consider specific prophecies that relate to man's inventions during the last days.

The Automobile In Prophecy

The first gasoline-powered vehicle capable of

transporting an individual for a distance of a mile or more appeared in 1887. The first marketable automobile with the capability of traveling faster than thirty miles per hour did not appear until 1900. But Adam could mount a horse and gallop through the Garden of Eden at thirty miles per hour. Thus, for fifty-nine hundred years, man was confined to traveling to and fro upon the face of the earth at this modest rate of speed. However, with the turn of the century a machine was put at man's disposal to propel him at speeds never before attained. Without the automobile, the industrial age would never have been possible.

The automobile has progressively become the symbol to man of his own personal pride and achievement. According to the 1989 edition of *The World Almanac*, there are over three million automobiles produced each month. Japan has surpassed the United States by making over six hundred fifty thousand automobiles each month; the U.S. is second with six hundred twenty-six thousand; and West Germany is third. In 1988 the automobiles of the world burned over twenty billion barrels of oil in their engines, the equivalent of eight hundred forty million gallons of gasoline. Even the present world oil reserve does not preclude the inevitable — one day soon the earth will simply run out of oil.

That the family car has a prominent place in the fulfilling of prophecy in the last days is beyond question.

1. The automobile has made any point within the radius of one thousand miles within a day's journey. Freedom

to travel in search of pleasure, knowledge, or business was not available in such abundance prior to the twentieth century. Without the automobile, the prophecy of Daniel 12:4 could not have been fulfilled: *"But thou, O Daniel, shut up the words, and seal the book, even to the time of the end: many shall run to and fro, and knowledge shall be increased."*

2. Bible prophecy projects that the Middle East will become of primary importance to all nations. We read in Zechariah 14 and Revelation 19 that the armies of all nations will merge in this particular area of the world at the battle of Armageddon. In Ezekiel 38 and 39, it is foretold that God will put hooks in Russia's jaws and bring Gog down from the north. In these days, God is using oil to bring this prophecy to pass. There is more oil in the nations of the Middle East than any other place in the world. It will become more precious to all nations over the next decade. Each time we start our automobiles, whether to drive a few blocks to the neighborhood grocery store, or to travel several hundred miles for pleasure or business, you and I move the present generation nearer a date with destiny, the battle of Armageddon.

3. The chariots of nations are mentioned repeatedly in the Old Testament because they played an important role in warfare. God had to intervene to destroy the chariots of Egypt in the Red Sea. Therefore, we could expect Bible prophecy to make note of the chariots of men and nations in the last days. Twenty-seven hundred years ago, a Hebrew by the name of Nahum

was given a vision of the world as it would be at the time of the coming of Messiah to establish His kingdom on earth. He wrote on a scroll what he saw: *"The shield of his mighty men is made red, the valiant men are in scarlet: the chariots shall be with flaming torches in the day of his preparation . . . The chariots shall rage in the streets, they shall justle one against another in the broad ways: they shall seem like torches, they shall run like the lightnings"* (Nah. 2:3-4). "The day of his preparation" means, of course, the preparation of the world for the second coming of Jesus Christ. The chariots of men today indeed look like flaming torches at night; they indeed justle against each other in the highways; and, they indeed run like lightning. Fifty thousand people are killed each year in the United States in automobile accidents. Since the turn of the century, more Americans have been killed in automobile accidents than were killed in World War One, World War Two, the Korean War, and the Vietnam War combined. The automobile is playing a prodigious role in the fulfillment of prophecy in these last days.

The Airplane In Prophecy

On December 17, 1903, Orville and Wilbur Wright flew the first airplane for a distance of one hundred twenty feet in twelve seconds at Kitty Hawk, North Carolina. The prophetic importance of this date is undeniable.

1. The airplane has greatly increased man's capacity to "run to and fro" over the face of the earth, as foretold by the prophets.

2. The airplane has made possible the prophecies relating to wars in the last days — nation against nation and empire against empire. Hitler's dive bombers brought into existence a new dimension of destructive warfare. The first atom bomb to be exploded in war was dropped on Hiroshima from an airplane. In the 1973 Yom Kippur War, the army of Israel was supplied by U.S. airplanes from bases eight thousand miles away. The battles to occur during the great tribulation would not be possible without the invention and development of the airplane as a weapon of war.

3. In World War One, British General Edmund Allenby was reluctant to bomb Jerusalem for fear of destroying the biblical sites, and according to reports, he read Isaiah 31:5: *"As birds flying, so will the Lord of hosts defend Jerusalem; defending also he will deliver it; and passing over he will preserve it."* General Allenby ordered his warplanes to fly over the city and the Turks surrendered Jerusalem without a shot being fired.

The Space Program In Prophecy

On October 1, 1957, Russia launched *Sputnik I* into an orbit ranging from one hundred forty miles to five hundred sixty miles above the earth. This earth-shaking event was followed two months later by sending a dog into orbit. Since that time, the United States has sent men to the moon and back; unmanned space probes have been sent to Mars and Venus; and fly-by missions have been sent to all other planets in our solar system. On the drawing board are plans to build cities in outerspace and colonize the heavens.

At Babel the human race combined its talents to build a tower to reach into the heavens. This seemed to be the answer at that time to a threatened catastrophe when the land mass of the earth broke up in the days of Peleg. God observed that man, whom He had made in His image, could do anything he imagined (Gen. 11:6). Today, the earth is again threatened by over-population, pollution, and nuclear destruction. As prophesied, man is saying again, "Let us go into heaven and make a way of escape." But, God will again intervene for the following reasons:

1. Wherever unregenerate man ventures, disease, plagues, murder, and war go with him. Man has ventured out into space, therefore war in heaven is being planned. The United States SDI defense plan is only the beginning for battle stations on other planets. The devil is now using man to help him in his evil scheme to elevate his throne above the throne of God. We read in Revelation 12:7 and 9, *"And there was war in heaven . . . And the great dragon was cast out, that old serpent, called the Devil . . . he was cast out into the earth, and his angels were cast out with him."*
2. In verse four of Obadiah, we read, *"Though thou exalt*

thyself as the eagle, and though thou set thy nest among the stars, thence will I bring thee down, saith the Lord. " The time of fulfillment of this prophecy is given in verse fifteen: *"For the day of the Lord is near. . . ."*

3. Moses prophesied in Deuteronomy 30:3-4 that at the time of the end, when Israel would be regathered, that even if any of God's earthly people had been driven out into the heavens, He would bring them back.

Only since the development of the space program within the past thirty years have we been able to comprehend the biblical prophecies relating to man's efforts in the heavens in the last days.

Radio and Television In Prophecy

On June 2, 1896, Marconi received the first wireless patent from Great Britain. On December 12, 1901, the first wireless messages were sent from Cornwall, England, to Newfoundland. The first television instrument capable of transmitting an image was produced in 1923. But God knew all about electrical communications thousands of years ago, even from before the creation of the world. We read in Job 38:34-35, *"Canst thou lift up thy voice to the clouds? . . . Canst thou send lightnings that they may go, and say unto thee, Here we are?"*

There are many prophecies that would have a doubtful fulfillment without the advent of mass communications. We read in Matthew 24:14, *"And this gospel of the kingdom shall be preached in all the world for a witness unto all nations; and then shall the end come."* The gospel is being preached into all the world today by means of radio and television. In the Greek language, *angel* means messenger. We read of a prophecy with a tribulation setting in Revelation 14:6-7, *"And I saw another angel fly in the midst of heaven, having the everlasting gospel to preach unto them that dwell on the earth, and to every nation, and kindred, and tongue, and people, Saying with a loud voice, Fear God, and give glory to him; for the hour of his judgment is come. . . ."*

We read in Revelation 13 that everyone in the world will see the Antichrist and all will be commanded to fall down and worship him. In Revelation 11:9 it is prophesied that all the world will see the bodies of two of God's witnesses lying in the streets of Jerusalem. These prophecies are now understandable in the light of the electronic miracle of television.

The Computer In Prophecy

Primitive computers were first used in World War Two for the purpose of converting radar information into firing data for anti-aircraft artillery and naval guns. From that initial beginning, the computer has developed into an electronic marvel that virtually controls everything we do. If all the computers in the world suddenly went down, traffic lights would not change; banks would not open; grocery lines would stop; airplanes would not fly — all working, buy, and selling would come to a standstill. The world would practically go dead.

Almost two thousand years ago, the Apostle John received a vision from Jesus Christ, and in this vision he saw all the world doing business using nothing more than code marks and numbers. We read in Revelation 13:16-17, *"And he causeth all, both small and great, rich and poor, free and bond, to receive a mark in their right hand, or in their foreheads: And that no man might buy or sell, save he that had the mark, or the name of the beast, or the number of his name."*

Yes, I believe we are living in the last days. Jesus Christ could come at any time to translate His church from this earth to Heaven. Man's inventions today foretell the Lord's intervention tomorrow.

But surpassing all the amazing inventions of man is still the miracle of the new birth which occurs when a sinner receives Jesus Christ into his heart as his Lord and Savior. Will you allow this miracle to happen in your life today?

Chapter Two

Mesmerized By the Bear:
The Great Soviet Deception

by Don McAlvany

Planet earth seems to be spinning faster and faster with each week and month that passes as political, economic, and monetary turmoil not only increases, but the *rate of change accelerates.* It is not only the events which are taking place which are significant, but the tremendous speeding up or acceleration of these events which needs to be considered. It is said that man has amassed more knowledge in the past thirty-five years than throughout all prior history. One large super computer can store quantities of information equivalent to thousands of years of prior knowledge and research, and process more data than all former computers combined. Instantaneous global communication today connects all points of the globe via satellite and other high technology, so that all events everywhere can be instantly known and viewed by everyone. A globe that once took months to circle can now be traversed in hours and every square inch of the planet can now be reached by destructive nuclear weapons within fifteen minutes, each with more explosive power than the world has seen in total prior to 1945. Isn't this acceleration of events, explosion of knowledge, and instantaneous global communications what we are told to expect in the "last days" scenario?

Geopolitical and world financial issues play an enormous role in end-time prophecy. Revelation 13 describes the beast that will have control over all buying and selling in the last days. This necessarily implies that the beast's governing political system will be in place to administer and enforce the financial system. This scenario not only appears to be developing, but also accelerating into place.

The acceleration or snowball factor can be seen in the deteriorating world debt pyramid where personal and business bankruptcies, S&L and bank failures, and Third World defaults are accelerating at a breakneck pace. It can be seen in the incredible upheaval and change in the Soviet Empire and in the accelerating communist revolutions in Central and Latin America, South Africa, the Philippines, and the Middle East. It can be seen in the stampede toward political, economic, and monetary union in Western Europe; and in the plunge toward a new world order and "the merger of the common interests of the U.S. and the U.S.S.R."

The U.S.S.R. is emerging as a major player in world developments today, but its true intentions are not understood by most of the world, including U.S. Christians. While the Soviet Union's role as Gog and

Magog per Ezekiel 38 and 39 is open to various interpretations, its current popular perception as an advocate of peace and brotherhood is total deception.

Jeremiah 6:14 tells of the people crying, *"peace, peace; when there is no peace."* In speaking of the last days, 1 Thessalonians 5:3 states, *"For when they shall say, Peace and safety; then sudden destruction cometh upon them, as travail upon a woman with child; and they shall not escape."* In his great end-time sermon in Matthew 24, Jesus describes great deception taking place that could even lead the elect astray. While perhaps not the final deception, great deception is taking place today.

Russian Dimitri Manuilski, in a speech to the Lenin School for Political Warfare in Moscow in the 1930s stated,

*"War to the hilt between communism and capitalism is inevitable. But today we are too weak to strike. Our day will come in thirty to forty years. **But first we must lull the capitalist nations to sleep with the greatest overtures of peace and disarmament known throughout history. And then, when their guard is dropped, we will smash them with our clenched fist.**"*

Is communism really dead? Is the cold war really at an end? Is Gorbachev really a great man of peace? Is the Soviet Empire really in its terminal crisis? Why have American leaders for over fifty years consistently helped the Soviet Empire grow and expand even as its leaders have promised to bury us?

What is really happening in the Soviet Empire? It is *not* disintegrating as the Western press keeps repeating. It is restructuring, rearranging, reorganizing, and rearming preparatory to its final thrust for world domination in the next five to ten years. Communism is *not* dead, as long as the Marxist-Leninist religion and dream of world conquest lives on in the minds of its leaders in the Kremlin. Gorbachev is *not* a great man of peace; nor is the cold war over as long as his military machine continues to grow to the most formidable size in world history and he continues to ship fifteen to twenty billion dollars in Soviet arms a year to Angola, Mozambique, Libya, Ethiopia, Afghanistan, Central America, and the Philippines while fanning a dozen wars of national liberation.

Mikhail Gorbachev is *not* a reformer, *nor* a closet liberal, *nor* a Christian, as the Western media tells us. He is the hardest core Marxist-Leninist since Lenin himself — the man former Soviet President Andre Gromyko described by saying, *"Behind the smile are teeth of iron."* In a speech to a large group of Russian students on November 15, 1989, Gorbachev said:

> *"We are for Lenin who is alive. . . . In building our future we are basing ourselves upon the gigantic intellectual and moral potential of the socialist idea linked with the theory of Marxism-Leninism. . . . We see no rational*

grounds to give up the spiritual richness contained in Marxism. . . .

"Through restructuring [perestroika] we want to give socialism a second wind and unveil in all its plenitude the vast humanist potential of the socialist system. To achieve this, the Communist Party of the Soviet Union returns to the origins and principles of the [Bolshevik] revolution, to the Leninist ideas about the construction of a new society. . . . Our Party was and remains the Party of Lenin. . . . In short, we are for a Lenin who is alive. . . . We must seek these answers guided by the spirit of Leninism, the style of Lenin's thinking, and the method of dialectical cognition."

Does this sound like a man who is presiding over the death of communism? The Lenin whom Gorbachev worships said: *"We advance through retreat"*; *"When we are weak, boast of strength"*; and *"When we are strong, feign weakness."* The old dialectical Leninist doctrine of taking two steps forward, and then one back to confuse the enemy is certainly being applied by his disciple, Gorbachev, today. It is called "scientific socialism" by the faithful, and of course Gorbachev has said that he does not want to discard socialism but to renew, restructure, and strengthen it.

At first glance, it seems as if the communist bloc is unraveling. But in reality, the Soviet Union is in complete control of the liberalization process and is simply meticulously following the *KGB script* laid out by Yuri Andropov and the KGB almost ten years ago. But there is a *second script*, a script being pushed by Western socialist leaders from Washington to Bonn to Brussels, and that script calls for a world socialist government (the new world order) by the end of this decade, which will merge the economic and political interests of America, Western and Eastern Europe, the Soviet bloc, and the Orient into one giant world socialist government (or dictatorship).

There is also a *third script*, one which is harder to define or quantify, but which is nevertheless coming to the forefront and that is the script of the New Age movement — an occultic, quasi-supernatural script which calls for a global government by the year 2000. All three of these scripts (conspiracies, if you will) have a target date of around the year 2000 for their respective forms of world government; all three parallel, overlap, cooperate, and mutually advance each other; all three (in the view of this writer) are distinctly different; and all three (in the view of this writer) have an evil, supernatural, satanic dynamic pushing them along. As things now stand, it would seem that some combination of these three scripts (or conspiracies) could succeed in establishing a global government before this decade is over.

A Tale Of Three Scripts

A. The Soviet Strategy in Europe — What is happening

in Europe today is an elaborate Soviet script (written almost a decade ago) to rearrange the European chess board in such a way as to shift the balance of world power, or correlation of forces, in favor of the Soviet Union by the end of this decade. Some of the key elements in this script are:

1. *Russia would feign economic collapse* — She is actually far stronger than the West is now being *misled* to believe as any close analysis of her military strength and production, her space program, oil, minerals, and industrial production would indicate. Soviet leaders have simply chosen to direct most of their economic energy into military expansion instead of normal economic endeavors. The Soviet and Western press complain about a shortage of soap and toilet paper, while the Kremlin builds a new multi-billion dollar nuclear submarine every thirty-seven days out of titanium which the Pentagon cannot afford.

2. *Russia would declare communism dead, the cold war over, and a new wave of democracy emerges in the Soviet Union and the Eastern bloc.* Communist Parties throughout the bloc would be innocuously renamed (i.e., Social Democrats, etc.), reorganized, restaffed with lessor known communists at the top, and secret police organizations "publicly" disbanded, but "privately" renamed, reorganized, and perpetuated. Opposing political grounds would be allowed to flourish, but would be infiltrated by the communists and the secret police. Rigged elections would be held

with much media fanfare. It should be remembered that the communists like to produce their own competition — a *fake* competition which they control (i.e., Solidarity in Poland). The name communism will fade from the scene and some name similar to Democratic Socialism will be adopted. All communists will call themselves "socialists" almost from this time forward.

The situations in Poland, Romania, East Germany, Czechoslovakia, Afghanistan, Angola, and Nicaragua are all far different than portrayed by the media. Common aspects include old communists reappearing as liberating leaders, secret police presence, and Soviet military presence.

3. *The Iron Curtain would be opened and the Berlin Wall dismantled* — The psychological impact of these moves on the West and the "illusion" of the collapse of communism was calculated by Andropov and company to almost totally eradicate the "threat perception" from the Soviets in the West. Much of this goes under the guise of *glasnost,* or openness and *perestroika,* or restructuring. Few remember that this has been used by the Soviets repeatedly over their sordid history.

The present period of *glasnost/perestroika* (the sixth since 1921) is designed to get America to disarm, to get the West to build up and bailout the Soviet Union economically and industrially, and to neutralize Western Europe and dissolve NATO. That this *glasnost* is a giant deception is easier to understand if one looks at it in the perspective of the first five Russian *glasnosts*, which were described in Edward Jay Epstein's book, *Deception* (Simon and Schuster, 1989).

The First Glasnost: 1921-1929 — Under Lenin's New Economic Plan, he persuaded Western governments, businessmen, and bankers that the revolution was "restructuring," moving back to the free market, and politically liberalizing. Massive Western financial and industrial aid poured in for nine years. *Glasnost* Number One ended abruptly in 1929, and tens of millions of Russians went to the wall shortly thereafter.

The Second Glasnost: 1936-1937 — Stalin suggested in the mid-thirties a restructuring of the Soviet economy along capitalist lines (he called it *perestroika*). He proclaimed that the Soviet Union was returning to a Western-style constitutional government, to freedom of speech, to freedom of assembly, and a return to free elections with secret ballots. Stalin was portrayed in the Soviet press and then the Western press as a pragmatist — not an ideologue (sound familiar?). Roosevelt and other Western leaders and businessmen, like the dog responding to Pavlov's bell, began to pour in billions in aid, credits, and trade. *Glasnost* Number Two came to an end abruptly in 1938, and the brutal purges known as the "Great Terror" followed immediately thereafter.

The Third Glasnost: 1941-145 — When Hitler invaded Russia in June 1941, the "partnership" with the United States was quickly revived by Stalin. Stalin again claimed that the militant phase of communism was at an end; he dissolved the Comintern (a key organ for spreading international communist revolution). He promised that after the war, Russia would be buying a massive amount of goods from the West. This all justified massive economic and military aid through the Lend-Lease Program (i.e., almost ten billion dollars). *Glasnost* Number Three ended abruptly in 1945, when the Soviets annexed the three Baltic states — Latvia, Lithuania, and Estonia, as well as parts of Poland, Romania, Prussia, Finland, Japan, and most of Eastern Europe. Over one hundred million people were enslaved and tens of millions subsequently died.

The Fourth Glasnost: 1956-1959 — In 1956, Krushchev launched another *glasnost* based on economic and political reforms, a return to competition and the free market, de-Stalinization, and a restoration of democracy and individual freedom in the Soviet Union. The Soviet press began to publish stories about private millionaires, underground businesses, and a thriving black market. Russian church leaders were allowed to travel abroad; Solzhenitsyn was allowed to publish his works; Soviet dissidents were allowed to have contact with the Western press. Krushchev complained about inefficiencies in the Soviet economy, and stated almost word for word, Stalin's earlier message to the West: *"If we cannot give our people the same standard of living that you give your people under the capitalist system, we know that communism cannot succeed."* Sound familiar? This is almost exactly what Gorbachev has been saying and doing. *Glasnost* Number Four began to end in 1959, with the Soviet-backed communist takeover in Cuba, the shooting down of an American U-2, the mass arrest of Soviet dissidents, and the erection of the Berlin Wall.

The Fifth Glasnost: 1970-1975 — The fifth *glasnost* was detent, initiated by Leonid Brezhnev. It offered to restrict strategic arms, negotiate mutually beneficial accords, and relax internal tensions. The Soviets began "public airings" of issues to explain to relevant audiences in the West why they had abandoned their prior goal of world revolution. The central theme of this *glasnost* was that the Soviet government was no longer run by ideologies, but by technocrats who had no interest in adhering to the Leninist doctrine of class warfare. Instead, like technocrats in the West, they wanted to expand their industrial base. The chief goals of this *glasnost* were to obtain increased U.S. aid and trade (which they did under Nixon and Kissinger), and most importantly, to inaugurate the arms control process. During this *glasnost*, Brezhnev appeared willing to let communist countries in Eastern Europe follow their own independent relations with the West, he announced unilateral troop cuts in Soviet forces in Eastern Europe. The Anti-Ballistic Missile Treaty of 1973 was one of Brezhnev's trophies from this *glasnost*. *Glasnost* Number Five began to lose credibility in 1975 when the Soviet-backed North Vietnamese overran South

Vietnam in violation of Russian promises to Kissinger. Over the next few years, widespread arrests of Soviet dissidents, resumption of covert actions abroad, and, finally, the invasion of Afghanistan in late 1979 by Russia, totally discredited this *glasnost.*

4. *The Soviets would launch the most spectacular disarmament campaign in history* — "publicly" making great concessions, signing the INF treaty and the START treaty, and then massively cheating on these and all previous treaties, while professing to be abiding by the same. Only gullible Western belief in elements one through three above would entice the West into massive disarmament while the Soviets continue the most massive but clandestine arms buildup in history. For example, during the entire eight-year Reagan "military buildup," the Soviets in actuality out-produced the U.S. in key weapons by the following ratios: intercontinental missiles — 4½ to 1; air defense missiles — 6½ to 1; bombers — 4 to 1; tanks — 3½ to 1; artillery — 8½ to 1. The Soviets are producing a nuclear submarine every seven weeks. Even though they received great acclaim for moth-balling four over-aged submarines in the Baltic, they still have four hundred fifty submarines to our one hundred forty. They are producing sixteen thousand SAM missiles per year and have massive superiority in tanks, anti-tank weapons, manpower, chemical weapons, artillery, combat aircraft, helicopters, as well as in tactical nuclear and ballistic systems.

5. *The Soviets would allow East and West Germany to*

reunite — but only if a united Germany becomes neutral, pulls out of NATO, and allows Soviet troops to remain stationed on its soil. Since Germany is the key country in NATO, her withdrawal would cause the collapse of NATO and all of Europe would become neutral and Finlandized. By way of explanation, Finland was a country which Stalin permitted in 1949 to do everything it wanted, while remaining as much at Stalin's mercy (via vast military intimidation) as any part of Soviet territory was. To be at a dictator's mercy cannot be called freedom in the Western political sense. Finland was given its special status because of Stalin's permission and the military Sword of Damocles the Soviet had over its head. Finland almost always votes with the Soviets in the U.N. A neutralized, disarmed, post-NATO Western Europe will be similarly Finlandized.

Once German reunification has occurred, Russia will make a major effort to separate Germany from the rest of its Western neighbors politically, militarily, and psychologically.

6. *America would be pressured to pull all of its troops and armaments out of Western Europe* — in the new post-cold war, post-communism era of European neutrality. Pacifist European governments and populations would demand such a pullout and leftist/communist pressure in the European and U.S. media and Congress would make such a U.S. pullout a *fait accompli*. Indeed such pressure in Europe and America has already begun.

7. *America and the West would come in and financially bail out the "newly democratized" Eastern European states and the Soviet Union itself* — America and Western Europe will pick up the forty to fifty billion dollars a year tab for financing Eastern Europe formerly paid by Russia. Direct U.S. financial aid to Russia has already been proposed in the U.S. Congress and by certain establishment types. U.S. banks, I.M.F., and world bank credits to Russia are beginning to flow, and over the next five years over one hundred billion dollars in credits and business projects in Russia will be injected by the West.

8. *High technology transfers from America and the West would accelerate* — in light of elements one through five above. Much of Russia's high technology has come from the West (bought, borrowed, given, stolen, etc.). America built the highly acclaimed Kama River truck factory for Russia in 1972 and Bush is busy modernizing it for Gorbachev today. It produces three hundred thousand military vehicles per year. Nixon and Kissinger pushed through the sale of America's ball-bearing technology in the early 1970s which allowed the Soviets to produce MIRVed (multiple warhead) missiles. Soviet espionage stole the U.S. secret to the atom bomb detonator and the U.S. technology on our nuclear submarines running silently. Now new Russian subs run silently and are therefore difficult or impossible to detect.

    The Soviets did not just fall off the turnip truck technologically. (Never underestimate your enemy!)

They lead America in space and in many areas of weapons technology, and graduate ten times more scientists and engineers than America does each year. But they hope to make some quantum weapons breakthroughs in the 1990s in post-nuclear weaponry which they are currently developing with new high technology from Japan, Europe, and America — breakthroughs which could seal America's fate once and for all. The Soviet hierarchy believes that the key to world domination is unlimited access to Western science and technology.

9. *NATO and the Warsaw Pact would be dissolved* — and an all-European security force combining the armies of Eastern and Western Europe would be formed. Of course, Russia would be the dominant military factor in all demilitarized Europe, and would then Finlandize the balance of Europe. Western Europe would have to be completely denuclearized in this scenario (and is moving rapidly in that direction at this writing).

10. *Eastern and Western Europe would be merged into one common European home* — This merger would first be economic, and then political. A united Europe would be neutral, socialist, Finlandized, and would exclude the U.S. economically and militarily. Soviet policy has never wavered from driving the U.S. (their ultimate enemy) out of Europe and isolating America. Gorbachev and "the script" visualize one socialist union from the Vladivostok to the Atlantic — dominated by Russia of course.

11. *The Chinese threat to Russia's southeast would be neutralized by the signing of a Sino/Soviet non-aggression pact* — Such a treaty is presently being negotiated and some partial agreements have already been signed.
12. *With Russia's western and eastern flanks neutralized, America excluded from Europe, disarmed, and demoralized, Russia would be free to move militarily into the Persian Gulf to dominate the Persian Gulf oil fields.* This will be partially precipitated by an emerging Soviet energy crisis.

The Soviet Union, the world's largest oil producer, produces about twelve million barrels a day and exports almost four million, including about two million to non-communist nations. But now the Soviet Union's energy crunch has begun, with a fuel crisis disrupting communications in Siberia and more than one hundred factories in Georgia forced to close for lack of oil. Russia's northern oil deposits are being immobilized because workers cannot reach the oil fields to maintain their equipment in temperatures of minus fifty degrees centigrade. Many oil wells have frozen over.

Oil production is down all across the Soviet Union and the Russians are not finding new reserves. They have no technology comparable to what the U.S. uses in Alaska to pierce the permafrost.

According to Radio Liberty analyst Leslie Dienes, seventy to ninety-six percent of West Siberia's oil production has come from five large oil deposits — all of which are in the last stages of their life cycles. So, like America, Soviet oil reserves are running down, some reserves are prohibitively expensive to produce, and by the end of the decade, Russia will be in a major energy crisis. Where can she look for abundant, cheap, and easy to produce oil reserves? To the south — to the Persian Gulf.

That is part of the Brezhnev Doctrine (1973) to seize the two treasure chests upon which the West depends: The Persian Gulf oil fields and the strategic minerals of South Africa. When that happens, the West will have been checkmated and the *de facto* surrender (it would innocuously be called "accommodation") of the U.S. and the West would in all likelihood follow.

This move on the oil fields by Gog and Magog suggests a soon fulfillment of Ezekiel 38 and 39. Different Bible scholars debate the timing of this, in terms of the whole end-times chronology. This move could also be part of the "Armageddon Scenario" (Rev. 16:16).

The above twelve-part scenario is the KGB script for Soviet world domination *by the end of the 1990s*. It was first written about by two former KGB officials: Anatoliy Golitsyn, about a decade ago, and published in his book, *New Lies For Old* in 1984; and Ion Pacepa in his book *Red Horizons*. These former KGB operatives believe that "the script" is intended to rescue and expand Eastern Europe and Russia's tyranny, convert it into a Euro-socialist communist tyranny; and then into a universal socialist tyranny via: a unified Europe; an all-European common market; and finally, a new world order.

B. The Push For a New World Order—

> *"We at the executive level here were active in either the OSS, the State Department, or the European Economic Administration. During those times, and without exception, we operated under directions issued by the White House. We are continuing to be guided by just such directives, the substance of which were to the effect that* **we should make every effort to so alter life in the United States as to make possible a comfortable merger with the Soviet Union"** (H. Rowan Gaither, President of the Ford Foundation — 1953).

> *"In politics, nothing happens by accident. If it happens, you can bet it was planned that way"* (Franklin D. Roosevelt).

> *"U.S. President Bush and Soviet President Gorbachev arrived yesterday on this Mediterranean island for a summit conference beginning today during which both hope to start the search for a* **new world order** (*New York Times*, Dec. 12, 1989).

America is run today by people from what this writer calls the Liberal Eastern Establishment. Made up of some of America's wealthiest finance capitalists (i.e., the Rockefellers, Andreas', Hammer's, and hundreds more), and certain liberal leaders in the media, the military, academia, and politics, this group dominates both U.S. political parties, the largest U.S. banks, and multinational corporations, and has as two of its prime U.S. political organizations the Council on Foreign Relations and the Trilateral Commission. This establishment group has controlled U.S. foreign policy since the 1920s, and liaises closely with the British Fabian Socialists, the Bilderburgers, the Socialist International, the Club of Rome, and other international groups who are working for a one world government. Their catch phrases for world government are "new world," "new world order," "one world," etc.

This group totally dominated the Carter Administration, had heavy influence in the Reagan Administration, and totally dominates the Bush Administration. Building up communist governments such as in the Soviet Union and the People's Republic of China, as a stepping stone toward world government and for megaprofits for the banking/corporate allies, is standard operating procedure for this group.

This group believes indeed that the "common interests of America and Russia can be merged" (like any corporate merger or leveraged buy-out), much as one of their minions, Rowan Gaither, said in 1953. That is why successive U.S. administrations keep pumping billions of dollars in aid and high-tech transfers into communist countries. Actually this group, and its now-deceased associates, have been financially supporting the Bolsheviks since before 1917.

Alexander Solzhenitsyn has said of this group:

> *"There also exists another alliance — at first glance a strange one, a surprising one — but if you think about it, one which is well grounded and easy to understand. This is the alliance between our communist leaders and your capitalists."*

These groups are comprised of socialists who not only look on freedom for the masses with disdain, but who would feel comfortable running Big Brother's Orwellian system described in *1984*. They are pushing for massive socialist legislation in America, for an end to financial privacy and ultimately a cashless society, and for a series of regional governments around the world (probably three) leading toward the new world order by the turn of the century. The United States of Western Europe is emerging in 1992 as one of those; the North American Common Market, including Canada, the U.S., and Mexico is another; and a Japanese/Pacific Rim Community will be the third. This corresponds to Zbigniew Brezezinski's trilateral group of North America, Europe, and Japan. By odd coincidence, George Orwell's *1984* also had three regional governments: Oceania, Eurasia, and Eastasia.

The United States of Western Europe — Conceptualized by a French socialist, Jean Monnet, in the post-war years, the European Economic Community was born, evolved to the European Community and in 1992 will become the United States of Western Europe. This economic union is about to become a political union, pushed through and headed by Europe's most fanatical socialists and one-worlder's. This united Europe will be run *by* socialists, *for* socialists, and is seen as a quantum jump toward world government before the end of the decade.

George Bush and his establishment associates want America to join in the union. James Baker, speaking in Berlin on December 12, 1989, said:

> *"We are Europeans — we will create a new Europe on the basis of Atlanticism."*

America's liberal eastern establishment wants America to join, as a giant step toward the new world order which Bush and his associates speak of so longingly. As America enters, the name will probably be changed to Atlantic Community. Gorbachev and the Politburo want to join for all the economic, financial, and high-tech advantages the Soviets would gain, and for the leverage Russia would achieve over Western Europe. Gorbachev speaks longingly of a united Europe from Vladivostok to the Atlantic — "a common European home for all of us." Gorbachev intends to become the controlling partner in this new axis. A reunited

Germany would join and economically control the newly created Europe. Then a restructured Soviet Union could join and dominate them both.

All of Eastern Europe and Russia are likely to be part of the European union. Uniting all of Europe has been tried before. Imperial Rome tried to unite Europe by force, and failed. Napoleon tried twice to unite Europe by force, and failed. But now Europe is to be united voluntarily from the Atlantic to the Pacific. A united Europe is a key linchpin in much last days prophecy regarding the Antichrist and his domain.

The countries in the united Europe will give up a great deal of their national sovereignty. In France, for example, the surrender of sovereignty to Europe has created a situation where forty percent of France's laws now stem from Common Market directives rather than from the French National Assembly. The same loss of sovereignty would apply for other European members and the U.S. as well *when* we join. And that is *before* Europe is even fully functioning. Only Margaret Thatcher, of all major Western leaders sees the danger and is trying to keep Great Britain out. And the British socialists will probably remove her from power because of her opposition.

As Larry Abraham said in his *Insider Report* of March 1990, regarding the emerging new world order:

> *"All of Europe — not just Russia or the Eastern bloc — is in the process of perestroika, or 'restructuring.' The first step is already*

finalized with the 1992 common currency for the EEC. This will be followed by the gradual surrender of national sovereignty to the European Parliament.

"The so-called Warsaw Pact nations will remain intact but will ultimately join this 'Urals to the Atlantic' federation. Mr. Gorbachev calls it 'our common home.' These steps are being initiated with meetings and agreements with the Conference on Security and Cooperation in Europe (CSCE). Watch for this organization to take on increased importance.

"The U.S. and the Soviet Union will join together in a 'superpower' alliance to act as world cops for preserving and enhancing the new world order. I have called this process 'The Greening of the Reds.' It will include their participation in such things as environmental protection, the war on drugs, and terrorism. The broad scope of this cooperation was keyed by Mr. Gorbachev in his U.N. speech last December and will start to take shape with new agreements strengthening the role of the World Court.

"The new world order agenda has been pursued relentlessly since the end of World War Two with no interruptions in strategy and only occasional shifts in tactics. The final question we need to answer is, 'Is it really so

bad?' My unequivocal answer is yes. Yes, because in the process we will lose more of our freedoms and most of our wealth. As the Insiders' age-old dream of a new world order comes closer and closer to realization, our personal options will be narrowed. We will, as Carroll Quigley said in Tragedy and Hope, *'be numbered from birth' and 'be followed through life.' It is George Orwell's nightmarish vision of the future come true."*

Christians, on the other hand, can be excited that the likelihood of the return of the risen Savior and King is imminent!

C. The New Age World Government — The New Age movement, a loose network of millions of people and thousands of organizations around the globe from environmentalists to occultists to satanists, believe their "christ" (not the Jesus Christ of the Bible) is alive and well on planet earth today and will soon reveal himself. The New Agers talk of a global government by the year 2000 and their government sounds like the socialist global government of the new world order crowd, replete with computers and other high-tech devices to control the over-populated masses.

Some New Agers believe that one-third of the world's population, who cannot adjust to their new program (i.e., about two billion people) will have to be terminated (i.e., killed). Before one totally dismisses the

New Agers as irrelevant kooks, it should be remembered that their belief system sprang from an Indian-Hindu sect, and is almost identical to the occultic beliefs which permeated and energized Adolf Hitler and the Nazi's Third Reich.

Many New Agers are also part of the new world order movement, high up in the liberal eastern establishment, and bring with them an occultic dimension to their socialist/globalist views. For example, Zbigniew Brezezinski, one of the three founders of the Trilateral Commission and an establishment leader in the new world order movement, is said to be a prominent New Ager.

This script is adequately described elsewhere in this book, so no need to extend discussion.

Conclusion

The Club of Rome is one of the most powerful and influential of the elitist one-world groups. The Club states that "only a global revolution, the substitution of a new world economic order can save us." THE COR intends to control international trade, world food, world minerals, and ocean management (*H. Du B. Reports*, Apr. 1985).

The COR is pushing for a cashless society. The book, *Microelectronics and Society: A Report To the Club Of Rome*, edited by Friedrichs and Schaff, states:

"The move to the cashless society seems

inevitable, given the technological push provided by microelectronics and significant cost advantages associated with the transfer of funds electronically."

The imposition of the cashless society is riding on the crest of a dual wave of counterfeit currency prevention hysteria and drug-war hype. The argument goes that drug lords operate with laundered money so "money laundering" is being used as an excuse by "Big Brother" to eliminate cash transactions, monitor all financial transactions, eliminate Swiss banking privacy, and neutralize all offshore tax havens. It would seem that if there hadn't been a drug war, one would have had to have been invented. Ron Paul very succinctly describes the concept:

> *"The new federal felony of money laundering is the crime of using your own cash, honestly earned and voraciously taxed, without filling out a federal form. The money laundering laws say nothing about drug profits. **Their real purpose is to stamp out the use of cash for reasons of government control and taxation."***

One does not need much imagination to see this cashless society fulfill the Revelation 13 beast economic scenario.

On April 18, 1980, the *Calgary Albertan* carried an article entitled "Club Of Rome Says: Messiah Needed."

In the article, it relates:

> *"[Aurelio Peccei (now deceased)] founder and president of the COR stated that 'a charismatic leader — scientific, political, or religious — would be the world's only salvation from the social and economic upheavals that threaten to destroy civilization. Such a leader would have to override national and international interests as well as political and economic structures in order to lead humanity away from the maladies that afflict it.'"*

Could that charismatic leader be Gorbachev — the most popular man in Europe and in the world today? Could it be the Antichrist? Whatever the answer, the 1990s promise *not* to be dull! The 1990s appear to this writer to be the decade of destiny. Three world governments aspire to, and believe they can install a global government on or before the year 2000: world communism; the new world order; and the New Age movement. All three cooperate, overlap, and link together, and all three movements have an evil, anti-Christian, satanic dynamic behind them. Christians need to awaken, to be alert to these movements, to take a stand against evil and for Jesus Christ in an exciting period which could be the countdown to Armageddon!

Chapter Three

The Creation Model

by Carl Baugh

In research conducted at the Creation Evidences Museum, some very unusual and startling things have been found that not only fit into the creation model, but that also show that things are winding up.

I have no doubt that we are living in the last days. By last days, I would like to specify that I am not referring to the earth turning into absolute chaos or the end of time. By last days I refer specifically to the fact that prophecy is being fulfilled, the Word of God is being vindicated, and there are signs that support the biblical precepts given regarding the last days.

These last days concern the winding down of the time of the Gentiles and the restoration of the nation of Israel. But specifically in eschatological study, they concern the return of Jesus Christ. By the return of Jesus Christ I am referring to two events. One event is the secret translation of the saints — the rapture. The other event is the return of Jesus Christ in glory. Both are in one view, particularly in the Old Testament, and both are delineated specifically in the New Testament as events related to the Blessed Hope. And it is a blessed hope.

We need the return of Jesus Christ. If we have had anything evidenced in recent years, it is that we are incapable of regulating and ruling ourselves. The earth is in such turmoil that we need the return of the Son of God. We long to see His face personally, and we long to see Him in charge of the events of the world.

I am quick to add that He is in charge in the full array and panorama of creation and the display of the universe. God is in the heavens. If we understand that, all is right in the heart, even though all is not right in the world. And we are certainly lying in the lap of the wicked one.

During recent years, prophetic exegetes (individuals who are scholars relative to eschatology — the doctrine of future events) have been very clear in the fact that prophecy is converging in that central event called the return of Jesus Christ. When we speak of the last days, we are speaking of the fact that this world is evidencing lack of control, evidencing prophetic fulfillment, and evidencing the time of the Gentiles in full display when their head of gold, which became in turn a bust of brass, a torso of iron, and feet of iron and clay, is near to being broken.

Satan himself is aware of all this, and is taking advantage of it. He is, by his lion-like energies, attempting and succeeding to some degree, to cause the revolt and animosity of the world against Christ Himself. There is a worldwide movement designed to alienate the Word of God, to neutralize the Word of God, and to persecute any concept relative to the literal Christ, the historic Christ, the living Christ.

It is amazing that Christianity is unique. Enfolded in Christianity is, of course, the historic Judeo position and the Old Testament scriptures, which are certainly the Word of God. Enfolded in the realm of Christianity is the Old Testament revelation and the historic prophecies. Now we find evidenced a specific animosity toward Christianity. And not simply toward Old Testament Judaism, but specifically against its revelation of Christ — Jesus Christ of the gospels and of the revelation of the New Testament.

It is the uniqueness of Christianity which in these last days has received absolute animosity. It is the uniqueness of the person of Christ that is rejected. Religious background is not rejected to any major degree, because even humanists admit that they are religious. They are attempting to devise and propogate a religion of global proportions encompassing the entire cosmos as manifesting itself in the final god called man. There is no scientific evidence for this whatsoever, but there is historical evidence that this is the philosophy and the religion of this hour. Anything that speaks of the literal uniqueness, the veracity, the viability, and the verified position of Christianity, and especially of Jesus Christ, is opposed in this hour. This is a spirit of antichrist that the Apostle John referred to.

Exegetes in the past have brought out ten specific signs that indicate that we are living in the last days. I will briefly list these ten things and give specific attention to additional areas which, in our research, have been both alarming and encouraging.

1. *The explosion of scientific knowledge* (Dan. 12:4). In this scripture, it states very clearly that knowledge shall increase. The original word used for increase in this scripture means "an exponential increase" — an explosion of knowledge. It is evidenced by our computer and space technology. Approximately every three years, we double our knowledge of the earth and of the universe. We are definitely having an explosion of knowledge.
2. *Spiritual decay* (2 Tim. 3:1-7). This is evidenced and pointed to by exegetes in prophetical study. The scripture reference gives a clear statement regarding the spiritual decay which is to be evidenced in these last days.
3. *Doctrinal apostasy* (2 Pet. 2:1). This is more evidenced than ever has been previously. Those who stand in the pulpit in liturgical concept are bringing forth doctrines that could be easily described as humanistic, because they certainly are not historic Christianity.
4. *Anti-supernaturalism* (2 Pet. 3:3). This is an amazing parallel of concepts. On one hand, modernists and liberals deny the supernatural nature of the Word of God. On the other hand, they espouse supernatural intervention in a cosmic context as if the universe were expressing itself, realizing itself, and from a distance imposing its own self-conscience on us here on planet earth. The scripture in 2 Peter 3 evidences this as

prophetic teaching within the Word of God.

5. *Conflicts between labor and capital* (James 5). It appears that not only within free societies but behind iron curtains, there have been recent revolts academically and economically. We have a perpetual conflict between labor and capital.

6. *World government and religion* (Rev. 3:7-8). There is a united effort to amalgamate the religions of the world into one cosmic religion — the religion of humanism.

   There is also an attempt to unify all governments into one world government. Individuals who study history and current events will certainly recognize that we have a revival of the Roman Empire in the European Common Market. Within this economic community in the last few years a currency has been devised and is ready to be extended to the global market.

   We have been rather amazed in recent months that *glasnost*, the new thinking behind basic communism, is becoming more global and is embracing more of our own concepts than we previously thought they would. We are marching pell-mell toward a climax of world government. The stage is clearly set.

7. *Materialism and secularism* (Luke 18:8). We evidence at every hand not only communistic nations becoming more materialistic, but our own people who have in the past embraced a spiritual concept and conviction, are now becoming more materialistic and secularistic than ever before.

8. *Worldwide famine and wars* (Luke 21; Matt. 24). I was

amazed recently when the captain of an Exxon tanker off the coast of Alaska that ran aground could affect you and I at the pumps, in our employment, and in the cost of living in every realm here in the United States, and internationally as well. The actions of one man, the captain, had global consequences. The events of his life have catapulted the price of oil on a global scale. In other words, what affects a part of the world affects all the world.

This point has been evidenced recently by claims that our ozone canopy is being depleted. Environmentalists report an increase of carbon dioxide and a warning of the global ecology to the point where our weather patterns are absolutely unpredictable. And we have pestilences on a rapid increase because of this. Matthew 24 certainly enumerates this among many of the signs that would be in the last days. Recently it was announced on a national radio broadcast that one of the problems with our chlorofluorocarbons (CFC's) that are damaging the ozone canopy and causing it to precipitate, or dissipate is that there is not enough charge in the upper atmosphere. We within scientific creationism have been forecasting this for some time. Dr. Thomas Barnes, a leading physicist, found several years ago that every fourteen hundred years the earth is losing half the energy in its electromagnetic field. The real problem is not simply the CFC's; the real problem is that we are losing the energy up where the ozone canopy is in effect. We are losing that energy to such a degree that any chemical arrangement would be an errant chemical arrangement. The Son of God, Jesus Christ Himself, certainly knew this would be the case well in advance, because He is the Creator who went to the cross. He is the Author and Finisher of the universe, as well as the Author and Finisher of our faith. He is the one who knows all thigns. By Him all things consist. Certainly He is aware, and has been since eternity, of the effects relative to His creation. Time and space are no problem for Him. So He would certainly be aware of the fact that the loss of the electromagnetic field after the drastic changes precipitated by the worldwide flood of Noah's day would endanger the lives of individuals in these last days.

Recent broadcasts have listed the fact that small botanical life forms and small creatures, insects in particular, would be drastically affected by the increase in ultraviolet radiation. The mutational variation caused by this new alarming rate of ultraviolet radiation will cause them to leave ecological bounds. They are already doing that. Some examples are the fire ant and the killer bee. Certainly we have a prophetic fulfillment forecast by none other than the Master of the universe Himself. I am convinced that we are living in the last days.

9. *The restoration of the nation of Israel* (Luke 2!). This passage shows that the nation of Israel will be revived toward the end of the "times of the Gentiles." The nation of Israel has been regathered. We are well aware of that. The nation of Israel is God's timepiece

and they are in preparation. I would specifically call your attention to the fact that Israel is now being isolated more than ever in the history of the world. Israel had a friend in the last half of the twentieth century — the United States of America. While Israel is currently still an ally of the United States, to an alarming degree Israel is being isolated by individuals and bureaucracies in the United States. This is to our detriment as a nation, because the Bible says that God will love those who love Israel, and curse those who curse Israel.

10. *Russia* (Ezek. 38; Rev. 13; Dan. 7). In these scriptures there is an amalgamation of the concept of a power, a god of forces, which we call Russia. Russia is listed in the Old Testament and is envisioned in concept in the New Testament.

The Creation Model

In research conducted at the Creation Evidences Museum, and particularly on research into the creation model, we have researched the scientific areas which support the creation model in the past, in the future, and in the current prophetic detail.

In Revelation 16, the return of Jesus Christ in the last days is stated in verses fifteen and sixteen: *"Behold, I come as a thief. Blessed is he that watcheth, and keepeth his garments, lest he walk naked, and they see his shame. And he gathered them together into a place called in the Hebrew tongue Armageddon."* In verse seventeen the prophecy goes on to state, *"And the seventh angel poured out his vial into the air; and there came a great voice out of the temple of heaven, from the throne, saying, It is done."* Notice verse eighteen particularly: *"And there were voices, and thunders, and lightnings; and there was a great earthquake, such as was not since men were upon the earth, so mighty an earthquake, and so great." "And every island fled away, and the mountains were not found. And there fell upon men a great hail out of heaven, every stone about the weight of a talent . . ."* (Rev. 16:20-21). There are some details given here which only now on a global scale have found a fulfillment in background concept.

In recent years geophysicists have related to us that the internal temperature of the earth near the core was approximately six thousand degrees Fahrenheit. Within the last three years these geophysicists again measured the internal temperature of the earth and found that it is now in excess of twelve thousand degrees Fahrenheit. This is in excess of the surface temperature of the sun, which is rather alarming. Calculations would not indicate that the gravitational pull and the density within the core would be enough to generate such temperatures, which indicates that there are some thermonuclear reactions occurring.

In the scripture referred to in Revelation it is very clear that there is going to be an earthquake in the tribulation period forecast, which will be of such proportions never before experienced in the history of mankind.

Prophetical exegetes have for the last two decades referred to the fact that earthquakes are increasing at an alarming rate. This is not only because of our sophisticated recording techniques, but because it is a fact that the earth is in trouble. The mantle of the earth is becoming increasingly more fragile. The internal temperature of the earth is warming to thermonuclear proportions. Something has to give. This is in accordance with the alignment of the planets in 1982. This alignment did not cause global earthquakes, but it did cause some shaking and realignment within the platelets to some degree. With the increase in the internal temperature of the earth and the realignment of the platelets, an earthquake could certainly be forecast.

Seismologists indicate that in the near future, the San Andreas Fault in the western United States will evidence a major earthquake. Of course, they have been forecasting this for quite some time, but now with these global proportions within the earth approximating the surface temperature of the sun, it certainly looks like we are in for a major reshifting of the physical forces of the globe. This could certainly be evidenced by the earthquake forecast in Revelation 16.

In addition, we have another alarming problem. Within the earth temperatures are almost exponentially increasing; outside the earth the electromagnetic field is decreasing. This has caused a decrease in the ozone canopy. Ozone is generated in the upper atmosphere and absorbs much of the ultraviolet radiation coming in from the sun and from outerspace. Apparently this canopy of ozone was generated after the *raqiya* firmament collapsed in the days of Noah and created the worldwide flood. This current content of ozone shielding has given us prosperity and benefits physiologically as well as economically, for the following reason.

We understand that as the ultraviolet radiation streams in at an alarming rate, it causes mutational variations on the skin of the human anatomy, which is, of course, cancer. This mutational variation is then introduced to the bloodstream, organs, and deep tissues of the body. We are all aware of the problem with cancer. The Environmental Protection Agency has announced that in the upcoming decades, one out of every three people worldwide will die from cancer induced by the increasing rate of ultraviolet penetration.

The basic reason for the loss of the ozone canopy is not the CFC's. The chlorofluorocarbons are certainly contaminating and helping to precipitate chemical compounds which neutralize the ability of this ozone canopy to filter out much of the ultraviolet radiation. But there is a deeper problem: the electromagnetic field is dissipating. This is the reason that the CFC's can penetrate and break down the ozone canopy. As the strength of that field dissipates, we are penetrated and violated by cosmic radiation, particularly the shortwave ultraviolet radiation.

Not only does it induce cancer and bring about holocaust within the ecospheres of planet earth, but recently published data indicate that this penetration of ultraviolet radiation will significantly damage small plants, small animals, and insects. They become variant and behave in bizarre ways. This is, of course, in keeping with the prophecies in Matthew 24 and the entire Book of Revelation where it is forecast that pestilences will be a tremendous problem in the last days.

Not only do these problems convince me that we are living in the last days, but today, for the first time in history, there is the scientific ability to fulfill the prophecy found in Revelation 13. In the latter portion of this chapter we have beasts out of the abyss which certainly form a model for beasts found in Revelation 9. These beasts in Revelation 9 were ridden by two hundred million militiamen from the East. In chapter nine, a description is given of these beasts, and in verse seventeen we find that they were horses, with breastplates of fire, heads of lions, and mouths issuing fire, smoke, and brimstone. In verse nineteen we find that they had tails like unto serpents which had heads. These were literal beasts ridden by literal militiamen who were invading the Middle East in the prophetic sense.

There have been numerous interpretations regarding this portion of scripture, simply because knowledge of this technology was not available until recently. Now, however, we are aware of various things occurring in the name of genetic recombinance — gene splicing. Scientists are now able to combine the genes of one life form created by our Designer with the genes of another life form created by our Designer, and from those original life forms produce a totally separate life form. In so doing, they are claiming to create life. Not so. They are simply recombining, in a bizarre way, the life that had a purpose and a balance in an orchestrated ecosystem designed for the benefit of man and the glory of the God of all creation.

Man is now able to play god to a marked degree by recombining the genetic code. Within nature, we have all the characteristics listed in Revelation 9. It is certainly within the realm of the knowledge of man to recombine the genetic code of one life form, splice it with another, come up with a bizarre life form, and then recombine that with another bizarre life form. It is certainly within the limits of scientific investigation and procedure today to come up with a creature that has the body of a horse, the face of a lion, the hair of a woman, and the ability to breathe fire. Thus, for the first time in history we have the ability to provide the context described in Revelation 9 and 13.

This brings us to a climactic statement in chapter thirteen which says that the head of a global empire, the beast himself, will be able to do a wonder. *"And he doeth great wonders, so that he maketh fire come down from heaven on the earth in the sight of men"* (Rev. 13:13). Satan is a master at taking advantage of and claiming the glory for that which originally was done by the Lord. In Revelation 13:13 we find that he had the ability to cause fire to descend from heaven at will. What is the explanation for this? In 1 Corinthians 15:51-52, we read, *"Behold, I shew you a mystery; We shall not all sleep, but we shall all be changed. In a moment, in the twinkling of an eye, at the last trump: for the trumpet shall sound, and the dead shall be raised incorruptible, and we shall be changed.* "Biblical scholars refer to this as the rapture, or the translation of the saints. It is prophetic chronology to occur at the beginning, or just prior to, the seven years of tribulation. At the end of that tribulation period Christ will return in glory. But now He comes in secret. Notice the Apostle Paul said, "I am going to show you a mystery. We are going to be changed in a moment, very quickly, as quickly as we can hear the words, 'Come up hither.' " Then he uses a special word in the Greek which translated says, "in the twinkling of an eye." We have often referred to this statement, believing that it meant the same thing as "in a moment." While that is true, the word in Greek suggests an even deeper meaning — the literal twinkling of an eye. The word is *repeto* and is the same word that is used for a nuclear explosion.

Can you imagine the living Son of God who is now again glorified, the Son of God whose appearance is as the sun shining in all its strength according to John's account in Revelation 1, coming into the atmosphere? In 1 Thessalonians it states that we shall meet Him in the air. Can you imagine the glorified radiant Son of God stepping into the atmosphere just long enough to say, "Come up hither"? Can you imagine His radiance as He catches us away?

His power is real. Yet His power is at that moment not a detonating, destructive radiance, but a beneficial radiance, much as it was on Mount Tabor, the Mount of Transfiguration when His raiment was as white as the light.

Can you imagine the Son of God stepping into the upper atmosphere to catch us away? The energy discharged would certainly recharge the electromagnetic field and would have effects that would be sensed worldwide. There would be evidence of the fact that there had been some radiation in the upper atmosphere. The recharging of the earth's electromagnetic field would be on a staggering level. Later, hailstones could be charged and weigh up to one hundred pounds because of the tremendous amount of energy in the electromagnetic field being extended to the particles of dust and water in the upper atmosphere. Thus, we have a background for that concept.

In addition, the Antichrist would certainly have scientific knowledge to be able to use that energy and to have an opposite plate put on earth. At his own discretion, within the sight of men he could appear to make fire rain down from heaven, when he is actually simply taking control of the work of Jesus Christ.

Scientific evidences show that our globe is headed for a date with prophetic destiny. We've all been aware of the general signs in the background, but now we are becoming increasingly aware that planet earth is in trouble, that conditions forecast specifically in detail within Old and New Testament prophecies are now ready to be fulfilled. I believe because of these and many other reasons that we are living in the last days.

Chapter Four

Ten Critical Issues

by David Breese

Nothing is clearer from the Word of God than the wonderful and comforting promise of the return of Jesus Christ to this world. In the light of that promise, none of the events, problems, joys, or disappointments of this world seem quite so important as once they did before we came to know the Savior. The person for whom everything is at stake and with whom everything is on the table in this life will certainly live in constant anxiety over the prospect of losing it all. The one, however, who lives in the hope of eternal life, which God who cannot lie promised before the world began — that person is infinitely less anxious about the affairs of this life. The best and the worst of this life is summed up by the Scripture, which calls it ". . . *our light affliction, which is but for a moment, worketh for us a far more exceeding and eternal weight of glory"* (2 Cor. 4:17). All of this life is but for a moment, and then the fading scenes of time must yield to the fadeless scenes of eternity's day. Christ is coming again — that promise is the blessed hope for all believers!

To properly understand the message of the Word of God which promises the return of Christ, we must remember that His return is spoken of in two different ways in Scripture. Or, if we please, the Bible promises that Christ is going to return "for His saints" (1 Thess. 4:17), and He is going to return "with His saints" (1 Thess. 4:13). The return of Christ with that army of His saints from Heaven will take place at the close of a period of time called the great tribulation (Matt. 24:21), at which time Christ will depose the Antichrist and set up His kingdom (Rev. 19:11-16). We therefore call this event "the glorious return of Christ," after which He shall reign to the ends of the earth and we shall reign with Him.

The occasion when Christ comes for His saints should be thought of as being very special to every Christian. That wonderful event will occur before the tribulation and will bring to pass the end of the church age. On that occasion, Christ will not literally come to the earth; rather, He will come to await us in the clouds. The Word of God gives us a most gripping picture of that event: *"For the Lord himself shall descend from heaven with a shout, with the voice of the archangel, and with the trump of God: and the dead in Christ shall rise first: Then we which are alive and remain shall be caught up together with them in the clouds, to meet the Lord in the air: and so shall we ever be with the Lord. Wherefore comfort one another with these words"* (1 Thess. 4:16-18).

Here we have an event which was not prophesied in

the Old Testament, as was the day of the Lord, and therefore needed to be especially explained to the church. The advent of the day of the Lord needed no explanation for those who were familiar with the Old Testament scriptures. About this, Paul immediately says, *"But of the times and the seasons, brethren, ye have no need that I write unto you. For yourselves know perfectly that the day of the Lord so cometh as a thief in the night. For when they shall say, Peace and safety; then sudden destruction cometh upon them, as travail upon a woman with child; and they shall not escape"* (1 Thess. 5:1-3).

This passage of the Word of God is followed by a most instructive promise made to Christians, of which we should take note. *"But ye, brethren, are not in darkness, that that day should overtake you as a thief. Ye are all the children of light, and the children of the day; we are not of the night, nor of darkness"* (1 Thess. 5:4-5).

So the Lord clearly informs believers that, if they pay attention to the Word of God, they can be aware of the approaching day of the Lord. Because the day of the Lord begins with the rapture of the church, to know of the advancing day of the Lord is a most reassuring hope indeed for believers.

We are living in such a time today!

Given the developments of this present age, every believer should certainly, in a new way, allow for the possibility that upon us has come the end of the world. In fact, this leads us to suggest the first reason why we believe that the coming of Jesus Christ for His church is a fast-approaching event. Yes indeed, one of these days we could well find ourselves caught up from the lesser pursuits of life and taken to be with Christ, to meet Him in the air. One of these days, we could be translated in a moment from this world into the world which is to come, from that point on to ever be in the presence of the Lord and to eternally participate in the joys and unimaginable fulfillments of Heaven. Why is this increasingly possible today?

The Critical Issues

The nearness of the return of Christ becomes a mounting reality when we consider the obvious fact that the hopes, dreams, and plans of this world are expiring fast. Let me suggest, in fact, that there are at least ten critical issues coming upon our generation which can no longer be ignored or avoided. A critical issue is one that, if allowed to mature, would end civilization as we know it today. These are not merely troubled times, but they are times in which the world is pressed upon by developments which could well write the expiration date of human history. These developments include the following:

1. *The dangerous confusion of the communist world —* There is every evidence that Marxist theory is now being seen as the nonsense that it has always been. But the breakdown of the communist world produces

new, wide instability across the face of the earth. We note also that, while shedding its satellites and admitting its economic weakness, the Soviet Union is involved in a crash program of military expansion. This has deadly implications for the future.

2. *The continued emergence of Islamic fundamentalism* — The Islamic world has been made fiercely volatile by the resurgence of the Shiite Moslem view within the world of Islam. The potential is that eight hundred fifty million followers of the prophet could be radicalized into a force that might attempt world conquest.

   The Moslems have two present ambitions. The first is to destroy the state of Israel, and the second is to conquer the world. The recent event of radical Moslems capturing and holding hostage the government of Trinidad is an illustration of this. The radical Muslims are gladly willing to die if they can kill some others and capture the world for the future of Islam.

3. *The new danger to the state of Israel* — Israel, with its three and a half million people, is now the object of mounting hostility by the Arab world. Fifty to sixty million people live in the nations immediately adjacent to Israel, and eight hundred and fifty million people live in the larger Arab world. Each of these has considered itself in a state of war with Israel, and a new call is now going out for a *jihad* — a holy war with Israel.

   In addition, a new wave of anti-Semitism is growing in Europe, the Soviet Union, and the United

States. Even the government of America appears to be turning from a traditional backing of the nation of Israel to a more neutral position.

4. *The Vatican factor* — The Catholic Church at Rome, with its seven hundred fifty million followers, has been aroused from the doldrums in recent years. Roman Catholicism is moving to become a new religious and political power broker in the world and is being accepted as such by a majority of the nations of earth. The recent book *The Vatican* explains the vast economic and political power of the Vatican and the corresponding moral force that it has in the world. This could trigger a global ecumenical movement, which is the hope and intention of many Catholics and Protestants. A unified world religion could become a part of the power of the Antichrist.

5. *Liberation Theology* — This new invention, this corruption of the Christian religion, has produced a semi-logical rationale to produce the unity of councilar Christianity and the Marxist/communist world. This prospect is made increasingly likely, for Liberation Theology has embraced one-half of world Catholicism along with the Protestant left and even the evangelical left. This new form of quasi-Christianity could become a major force in the overturning of the democratic concepts that have made Western civilization.

6. *The threat of global economic collapse* — The news of every new day brings increasingly alarming reports as to the immense debt of the United States — now the new debtor nation of the world — and also the

nations of the Third World, Africa, and Latin America. Now new billions of dollars of obligations have been poured upon the present government from the massive savings and loan crisis and the threat of the insolvency of six of the leading banks of the United States. America is sinking into a sea of red ink, while Japan and Germany are increasingly able to dictate the policies of the world. Indeed, the dreadful economic manipulations which have brought us to this unhappy impasse could well bring the advent of the third rider of the Apocalypse. He announces that a day's pay will buy a loaf of bread. This condition could instantly come upon the nations of the Western hemisphere.

7. *The AIDS pestilence* — The Scriptures indicate that one of the signs of "the beginning of sorrows" will be pestilence. Once upon a time, this would have been completely discounted by people of modern thinking who believe that medicine has the solution to every problem.

Now the AIDS holocaust is upon us in dreadful fashion. Eighty thousand homosexual men have died in the United States, and eighty thousand more can be expected to die within the next year. Even as we write, the current news announces that we have under-estimated the seriousness of the AIDS crisis and that a greater holocaust than ever is coming upon us.

AIDS is in a sense the disease that contains all others. It is the result of paying insufficient attention to the teaching of Scripture which says, *"Be not deceived; God is not mocked: for whatsoever a man soweth, that shall he also reap. For he that soweth to his flesh shall of the flesh reap corruption; but he that soweth to the Spirit shall of the Spirit reap life everlasting"* (Gal. 6:7-8).

8. *The threat of nuclear holocaust* — Within the hands of the nations of the world is the devastating explosive possibility of exterminating life in this world. On the United States' side, there are one thousand fifty *Minuteman III* intercontinental ballistic missiles. Superior numbers of these are in the hands of the Soviet Union and are aimed at major cities in the United States. Nuclear capability is also in the hands of England, France, India, Israel, China, and perhaps other nations.

Once the prediction of Scripture concerning devastation in the world was considered quite impossible. Now we know that these scourges could be brought to pass by the hand of man. The Bible says, *"And the second angel sounded, and as it were a great mountain burning with fire was cast into the sea: and the third part of the sea became blood; And the third part of the creatures which were in the sea, and had life, died; and the third part of the ships were destroyed. And the third angel sounded, and there fell a great star from heaven, burning as it were a lamp, and it fell upon the third part of the rivers, and upon the fountains of water; And the name of the star is called Wormwood: and the third part of the waters became wormwood, and many men died of the waters, because they were made bitter"* (Rev. 8:8-11).

All these dreadful possibilities are now within the realm of perverse human capability. The indication of Scripture is that, during the days of the great tribulation, they will in fact be used.

9. *The awful cost of conventional warfare* — The nations of the earth this last year spent one trillion dollars on armaments, preparing for war with somebody. This insane expansion of military capability could, of itself, not only kill millions of people, but also destroy the economic system of the world. Many nations that can least afford expensive military hardware are expending their resources on this rather than the welfare of their people. But because this is a sinful world, such cruel profligacy is inevitable.

10. *The decline of morality in the world* — Every believer knows that the basis of life is moral. When society experiences a breakdown of morality, that society cannot long survive. This condition is exactly predicted in the Word of God. "*. . . in the last days perilous times shall come. For men shall be lovers of their own selves*" (2 Tim. 3:1-2). As a result, "*. . . evil men and seducers shall wax worse and worse, deceiving, and being deceived*" (2 Tim. 3:13).

The Ultimate Foundation

Behind every other entity in society — commerce, government, education, international affairs — there must be a moral issue. Failing this, no society can endure for long. That moral base has now virtually disappeared in Western civilization. Do we dare note that therefore the only hope for civilization is in the spiritual area? A revival of the spiritual reality of historic Christianity can alone undergird the moral base without which society cannot long endure.

This moral breakdown is what could bring on exactly the conditions of the great tribulation. So deteriorating and ultimately evil will be those days that the Scripture says, "*. . . except those days should be shortened, there should no flesh be saved: but for the elect's sake those days shall be shortened*" (Matt. 24:22). Given this condition of our world, can such a day be far away?

These aforementioned critical issues are, it is to be remembered, dynamic rather than static. They continue to change, and they change on the growth side. All of the evils that they represent are becoming worse and worse.

How then can we ignore the fact that we are at the place where only Divine intervention can save us? It is a finite world, and therefore there must be a breakpoint for everything — a point where it can no longer support the degree of corruption that has come upon us. The remaining honest people in Washington and in the capitals of the world are admitting that we are at a place where nothing human can now save us.

How marvelous, therefore, that we have the promise of the return of Christ. Despite every one of the known deteriorations of our world, we Christians should continue to rejoice in the bright expectation of the return of Christ. How marvelous to remember that "*For God hath not appointed us to wrath, but to obtain salvation by our Lord Jesus Christ, Who died for us, that, whether we wake or sleep, we should live together with him"* (1 Thess. 5:9-10).

Speaking about a whole set of events such as these, Christ said, *"And when these things begin to come to pass, then look up, and lift up your heads, for your redemption draweth nigh"* (Luke 21:28).

What Shall We Do?

May we suggest this course of action for every child of God. Looking about us in a horizontal direction can only bring despair. However, looking up is another story indeed. Daily we should examine the skies and remind ourselves that "perhaps today" Christ may return for His own.

Now, of course, that places a real responsibility upon us. In that the whole world will one day pass away and in that most certainly we will pass from this world however long it endures, what manner of persons ought we to be in all holy conversation and godliness? As never before, we should be articulate witnesses for the Savior. We do well to take every opportunity to minister to people who may soon die and be lost forever. Explaining to them the marvelous message of the Word of God concerning the gospel and the tremendous hope of the return of Christ is a wonderful motivation for every man to come to the Lord Jesus.

Our own lives should also be consecrated to the

Savior. How foolish to live for the things that will soon be gone. How tragic it is that many people, even Christians, tend to sacrifice that which is eternal for the temporary fulfillment of indulging in that which is temporal. We are advised against this in the Word of God, and every sensible person knows that we are advised against such a course by our human experiences as well.

Therefore, in the midst of all of these things, let us look for our redemption that draws nigh. Looking for the return of Christ will not only produce bright anticipation, but the needed personal purity which the church must have today.

There is another development concerning which we must earnestly pray. The scripture says, *"We have also a more sure word of prophecy where unto ye do well that ye take heed, as unto a light that shineth in a dark place, until the day dawn, and the day star arise in your hearts"* (2 Pet. 1:19). That sure word of prophecy is, in our time, the best source of solace, hope, comfort, and motivating anticipation which the church has. The great need, therefore, with the church is for a renewed attention to the teaching of the prophetic Word. How dull is that concentration which only looks at today, seeking fulfillment, realization, and happiness within the historical process. Such concentration, so common within the ranks of Christians today, can be most debilitating. We are constituted so that we are to be motivated by hope, by anticipation. When will we learn that there is no final fulfillment available within the historical process?

But alas, one day the "historical process" will give way to the reality of eternity. Then shall we realize that we missed one of the great blessings of life, while we were in the scenes of time, by not paying proper attention to the prophetic Word. What purity, what godly witnessing, what spiritual effectiveness would have been created in the church down through the ages if it had paid the needed attention to the prophetic Word and perhaps less attention to the bricks, the stones, the organization, the stained glass, the artifacts of time. "Presentism" is a point of view which is becoming increasingly untenable. Rather, the Apostle Paul says that we are to be reaching forth to those things which lie before (Phil. 3:13).

There is no question about the fact that Christ is coming again! The probability of His return in our lifetime is increased with every day that passes. That probability is also strongly presented to us by "the signs of the times." Therefore, a person is not wise to refuse to look up. Rather, we should daily examine the clouds and say, "Perhaps today!"

Chapter Five

Israel, Armageddon, and World War Three

by Grant Jeffrey

For hundreds of years Christians have earnestly looked and hoped for the return of Jesus Christ. In every generation that has passed since the destruction of the Temple in 70 A.D., Israel has prayed for the coming of the Messiah and the rebuilding of the Temple. Are there any objective reasons that would convince us with logic, as well as hope, that we are living in the time that will see all the prophesied events of the Old and New Testaments, and the coming again of Jesus, first for His church in the rapture and then with His church in glory to set up a kingdom which will never end? I believe there are.

The first reason is the nation of Israel itself. God prophesied many times that if Israel were disobedient and rejected its King and His kingdom, He would disperse them throughout the world for many generations. Israel's history reflects that fate. After rejecting their Messiah and King in 32 A.D., the Roman army dispersed Israel throughout the known world within thirty-eight years. For hundreds of years no Jew was allowed to go within the walls of Jerusalem.

In Matthew 24, while standing outside the Temple, the disciples asked Jesus Christ: "What will be the sign of your coming again as Messiah and Christ?" Jesus gave them many signs that we, as students of prophecy, are very familiar with. One of the most significant is found in Matthew 24:32-34: *"Now learn a parable of the fig tree; When his branch is yet tender, and putteth forth leaves, ye know that summer is nigh: So likewise ye, when ye shall see all these things, know that it is near, even at the doors. Verily I say unto you, This generation shall not pass, till all these things be fulfilled."* Several times in the Old Testament (Jer. 24:1-5; Hos. 9:10), God used the symbol of the fig tree or figs to refer to Israel. In Matthew 24:32, Jesus is talking about Israel, who like a fig tree became barren, a nation lost in the graveyard of the other nations of the world for two thousand years. Aside from all the other signs of which we are familiar, Jesus said that the pre-eminent sign indicating the approaching last days was that the fig tree, Israel, would put forth its leaves. He goes on to say that the generation seeing this happen will not die, will not pass, until all the other signs have been fulfilled. Just before that, Jesus described not only the signs leading up to the great tribulation, but also the events of the great tribulation and Armageddon, when He will return with His church to set up the kingdom that will never end.

The question is: Was this prophecy fulfilled in the rebirth of the nation of Israel on May 14, 1948? Without question, biblical scholars agree that Israel was reborn in 1948, completely fulfilling this prophecy of Jesus Christ, and many other prophecies concerning Israel in the Old and New Testaments. In *Armageddon — Appointment With Destiny*, I point out that a unique prophecy in Ezekiel 4:4-6 in which Ezekiel was given a very strange prophetic injunction to lie on his side for three hundred and ninety days and then on his other side for forty days. Every day represented a year of punishment. Looking at these four hundred and thirty days in light of Leviticus 26 and the prophecy Moses gave to Israel that if they failed to repent after judgment, whatever had been promised them would be multiplied seven times, works out to conclude that Israel's captivity would end precisely on May 14, 1948. This prophecy is outlined in chapter three of the book and is incredible proof that God is sovereign, and by His glory He is manifesting this sovereignty throughout history by bringing these events to pass exactly on the appointed days. Against all the odds and thousands of years of predictions of desolation, Israel came back from the graveyard of nations and today stands upon the mountains of Israel, exactly as Ezekiel prophesied in 37:10 as ". . . *an exceeding great army.*"

In 1948 Israel had an air force of two captured Piper Cubs and an armored force of several jeeps. Yet, with God's help they defeated combined invasion forces of five Arab armies that attacked Israel simultaneously. Many miraculous stories were told from the victory that Israel won in that war, and again in 1956, 1967, and 1973.

Over and over again nations have tried to defeat Israel, but God has stood with them and defeated their enemies.

Today, Israel stands at the crossroads of history on the most strategically important piece of real estate in the entire world. If it were not for Israeli defense forces, I believe that long before now the Russians would have very easily attacked and conquered Saudi Arabia, along with other countries in that area, and taken over their oil fields. Because Israel stands with the military ability to defend her interests, as well as North America's, we still have dominant control of the area.

God predicted twenty-five centuries ago that after Israel was brought back to become a nation, He would raise up a country known as Magog. Ezekiel 38 and 39 states that God would cause Gog, the chief prince of Magog, to gather together an alliance of nations in a confederacy to invade Israel. Russia, known by Bible scholars to be Magog, is at present allied with the nations named by Ezekiel. Ezekiel identified these nations by giving the names of the sons and grandsons of Noah who settled in the areas now known as Eastern Europe, Russia, Ethiopia, Libya, and Persia, which includes Afghanistan, Iran, and Iraq. Each of these were listed by Ezekiel as being allied with Russia in the last days and participating in surprise attacks on Israel after she had become a nation. We see that precise alignment of nations today.

Ezekiel also prophesied that Russia will be "*. . . a guard unto them . . .*" an armorer for the nations allied with Russia (Ezek. 38:7). It is very significant that every one of those nations is armed by the Soviet Union. They all have AK-47 Klasnokov Russian assault rifles, Soviet armored personnel carriers and tanks, and Soviet surface-to-air missiles.

God continued to say that Russia and these nations would attack Israel, and He would defeat them. It will not be the United States, but God who will defeat them in the greatest military disaster in history, so great that God says it will take seven months to bury the dead. Enough fuel will be made from these weapons to last Israel for seven years. Many feel that with the modern weapons being made today, it would be impossible to burn weapons for fuel. Russia is using a material called lignostone, developed by Holland over twenty years ago, made of compressed wood. It is very similar to steel, but is lighter and harder than steel, yet when it is put into a furnace, it burns hotter than coal. This prophecy seems to be on the verge of being literally fulfilled.

When Israel invaded Lebanon in 1982 to destroy PLO bases, God allowed them to capture over five hundred thousand Soviet AK-47 assault rifles, hundreds of thousands of uniforms, together with K-rations and other military supplies. Documents were also found indicating these items had been buried in Lebanon as pre-positioned supplies for a forthcoming attack by Soviet and Warsaw Pact forces. The PLO, Lebanese-Muslim forces, Syrians, and Iraqis had far more weapons then they could possibly use. When the attack was launched, volunteers could be called from Eastern Europe and Russia, lightly armed and loaded onto planes, and upon landing in Syria, Iraq, and Lebanon, they could pick up the pre-positioned weapons and pour into the northern mountains of Israel. As a result of finding and confiscating these weapons, Israel is now a major exporter of Soviet arms, second only to the Soviet Union.

Russia did not change their plans; they simply postponed them. A Canadian, Sir William Stephenson, also known as Intrepid, was head of Combined Allied Intelligence operations during World War Two. He reported that in November 1987, Soviet President Gorbachev, in a speech to the politboro, made the following statement:

> *"Gentlemen, comrades, do not be concerned about all you hear about* glasnost *and* perestroika *and democracy in the coming years. These are primarily for outward consumption. There will be no significant internal change within the Soviet Union, other than for cosmetic purposes. Our purpose is to disarm the Americans and to let them fall asleep. We want to accomplish three things: One, we want the Americans to withdraw conventional forces from Europe. Two, we want them to withdraw nuclear forces from Europe. Three, we want the Americans to stop proceeding with Strategic Defense Initiative."*

The Soviets want these concessions from the United

States because they have been spending over twenty billion dollars each year for many years on their own Strategic Defense Initiative and have achieved some stunning breakthroughs. They know it has potential to at least limit an enemy attack.

Gorbachev reportedly also sent a letter several months ago to Yasser Arafat, the head of the PLO, in which he promised that sometime within the next several years, Russia would initiate some spectacular action on behalf of the Muslim cause concerning Israel and Jerusalem. This would prove to the Muslims once and for all that Russia is their best friend and supporter.

Today, Russia is allied with all the nations listed in Ezekiel 38 and 39. This is one of the many reasons which leads me to believe that we are the last generation. Jesus said the generation that saw the nation of Israel reborn would see everything else (Matt. 24:34). Therefore, all those living in 1948 can hope with reason, as well as faith, that within their natural life span they will see the return of Jesus Christ. I was born in 1948, and I believe this prophecy indicates clearly that we will see all of these things come to pass.

In Matthew 24:21-22, Jesus describes several things about this time period. He says, *"For then shall be great tribulation, such as was not since the beginning of the world to this time, no, nor ever shall be. And except those days should be shortened, there should no flesh be saved: but for the elect's sake those days shall be shortened."* Jesus Christ refers here to battles that will take place leading up to the battle of Armageddon. His words two thousand years ago, I believe, anticipate our nuclear age, with our weapons of mass annihilation, nuclear and hydrogen bombs, and chemical and biological warfare. For the first time in history, we have the capacity to destroy all life upon earth if all our weapons were unleashed in the same war. It is to our generation Jesus is referring concerning His return when He says: *"And except those days should be shortened, there should no flesh be saved . . ."* (Matt. 24:22). The ability to destroy the earth was not possible in the 1800s or the early 1900s. But since the creation of mass numbers of nuclear weapons, over sixty thousand in the world today, along with mass amounts of biological and chemical weapons in the armories of many nations, the world has the capability for self-destruction that requires Jesus Christ to intervene to save mankind from himself.

Christ also describes nation rising against nation. In the generation leading up to His second coming, nations would not fight only one nation against another, but treaties would cause many separate nations to form into large blocs, seen for the first time in this century. In World War One, almost every nation on earth became involved on one side or the other. World War Two followed the same pattern. Today, nations are divided between East and West. In a way, only the stars in the heavens are neutral. In the next war, it is difficult to realize how any nation will be able to escape involvement as they have in the past.

The Lord said there will be an increase in famines in the last days. In spite of the green revolution, famine is increasing. Starvation is such that over half the world's population goes to bed hungry every night. The problem is sin: mankind's evil has forced him into a no-win situation. The United States spends over two hundred times more on arms than on international food aid. We have the ability to feed the world, but we lack the political and spiritual will. Collectivization by Ethiopia's communist regime is only one example of a country which was a net exporter of food before the revolution in 1973 and is now a basket case. Even Russia under the czar in 1917 was a major exporter of grain. They are now a major importer and cannot feed themselves despite massive credit from the West, modern technology, and fertilization. The sinful plans of communism cause a man not to be able to reap the fruit of his own labor and have created such disincentives that Soviet and other collectivized farmers have no motivation to feed more than their own families. Famines are increasing, especially as they follow wars and civil wars.

Jesus continued to say there would be earthquakes in strange places. Seismology grafts show earthquakes increasing every year. Over one million earthquakes were registered last year. More than ten thousand were strong enough to be felt. Many were only tremors, but scientists say that the forces building up under tectonic plates are ready to be unleashed in many strange places around the world. The number of earthquakes above five on the Richter scale has more than doubled every decade since 1900. This is clearly a fulfillment of the prophecy in Matthew 24:7.

Christ said there will also be pestilences in the last days. Even with modern medicine, the world is afflicted again with malaria, smallpox, and other diseases that fifteen years ago were thought to have been eliminated. Sexually-transmitted diseases that ten years ago were defeated are returning with a vengeance. Over three million cases of different types of syphillis, gonorrhea, and other genital diseases are appearing in the United States every year.

AIDS is growing at an alarming rate throughout the world. However, the figures reported are only for those individuals who have come down with AIDS completely, having all the symptoms of the disease. The figures for those who test positive for the AIDS Related Complex are staggering. I have talked with doctors who predict that in Africa thirty to fifty million people will die from the AIDS virus alone in the next four years. This is a tragedy unparalled in history, including the Black Plague in the fourteenth century. Only one-third of those afflicted with the plague died. I believe that we are faced today with a pestilence in fulfillment of what Jesus Christ prophesied because mankind has chosen to break the laws of God, because he has chosen to do things his way. The result of the new morality, or immorality, is that fifteen sexually-transmitted diseases are rampant throughout the world. In Latin America, and in America itself, these sexual diseases are being followed by AIDS. AIDS is the first disease in history of which there are no cases of recovery, with no cure in sight. It is one hundred percent fatal. I believe Jesus

Christ was talking about just such a situation that would occur in the generation preceding His return.

Jesus went on to describe false prophets, how the love of many would wax cold, and how the gospel of the kingdom would be preached in all the world, and then the end would come (Matt. 24:11-14). In the last few decades, the gospel of the kingdom is being preached in all the world, not only on radio stations and programs like The Southwest Radio Church, but around the world in various media formats. Over three million Bibles were distributed last year. The latest statistics say that there are seventy-eight thousand new Christians each day, a figure not seen even in early New Testament times. There are seventy-six thousand missionaries in the world, with many native workers doing such a tremendous work that one thousand new churches are formed in Africa and Asia every week. The largest churches are in South Korea, with Rev. Yonggi Cho's congregation totalling more than five hundred thousand. In Santiago, Chile, one church has over a quarter of a million members. This has never been seen before in history. The gospel has now been translated into one thousand seven hundred sixty-three languages. Unreached ethnic groups have decreased to hundreds. We are on the verge of the fulfillment of the prophecy in Matthew 24:14.

Jesus also said, *"When ye therefore shall see the abomination of desolation, spoken of by Daniel the prophet, stand in the holy place, (whoso readeth, let him understand:) Then let them which be in Judaea flee into the mountains"* (Matt. 24:15-16). He was talking to the

Jews who will be upon the earth at the beginning of the great tribulation. Jesus is speaking of the Antichrist, who will commit the abomination of desolation when he goes into the holy place. Jesus had just come from the holy place, the Temple, and His disciples knew that He was referring to the Temple. From this prophecy and also many others, it is clear Jesus is stating that the Temple must be rebuilt before the Antichrist can go into it and desecrate the Holy of Holies. Israel is very close to rebuilding the Temple, which is a significant sign that we are quickly approaching the return of Jesus Christ.

Micah 4:1 states very clearly that in the last days the Temple is to be reestablished on the mountain of the house of the Lord. This refers to the court of the Gentiles and will exist in the last days. *"But in the last days it shall come to pass, that the mountain of the house of the Lord shall be established in the top of the mountains, and it shall be exalted above the hills; and people shall flow unto it. And many nations shall come, and say, Come, and let us go up to the mountain of the Lord, and to the house of the God of Jacob; and he will teach us of his ways . . ."* (Mic. 4:1-2). Other prophecies also state this, as in Amos 9. In 2 Thessalonians 2:4, Paul says that the Antichrist, the man of sin and the son of perdition, will go into a rebuilt Temple, sit in that Temple, and claim to be God. This prophecy can be fulfilled only if the Temple is rebuilt. Israel is very close to the rebuilding of the Temple, so close that we can hear the footsteps of the Messiah resounding on the hills of Judea. *"And when these things begin to come to pass, then look up . . . for your redemption draweth nigh"* (Luke 21:28).

The Temple was the central focus of Israel's worship for over three thousand years. It was built by King Solomon with the materials prepared by King David. The Ark of the Covenant was brought into the Temple to form the focus of Israel's worship system. The Temple was first destroyed by the Babylonians in 587 B.C. on the ninth of Av, the fast of mourning. On the same day, six hundred fifty-six years later, the Romans destroyed the second Temple, the one in which Christ worshipped in 70 A.D. on the ninth of Av. The Temple has remained in ruins for almost two thousand years. In May 1948, Israel was reestablished as a nation in fulfillment of the prophecies made by God many centuries ago. With the fulfillment of the prophecy of the rebirth of Israel, it became possible for Israel to rebuild the Temple.

In 1967, Israel recaptured Jerusalem, including the Western Wall and Temple Mount. Rabbi Shlomo Goren, chief rabbi of the Israeli Defense Forces at the time, ran to the Western Wall, which had been under Jordanian control from 1948 until 1967, with Israeli paratroopers and blew on the ram's horn. He was asked by the Israeli historian: "When will we rebuild the Temple?" He answered: "As it was in the days of King David, that within forty years of the capture of Jerusalem his son Solomon built the Temple, even so, it will be with us."

Israel has the Temple Mount in its possession. While they have allowed the Muslim police control upon the Temple Mount and the observance of religious services, many Jews in Israel are concentrating upon the need to reinstate Temple worship services. Thousands of Jews in Israel are not interested in the Temple. But there is a strong movement which recognizes the necessity to rebuild the Temple so that the Messiah will come.

There is a debate throughout Israel and the entire Jewish world. Many rabbis believe Ezekiel chapters forty through forty-eight very clearly describe the millennial Temple as the third Temple, an enormous project built by the Messiah. Zechariah also refers to a Temple built by the Messiah. Rabbis looking at these passages insist the Jews should not rebuild the Temple, but wait until Messiah comes. However, an increasing number of rabbis, Orthodox Jews, Levites, and Cohanene believe the Bible indicates they will build the Temple as the first two Temples were built. Then the Messiah will come. The reconciliation between these two differing viewpoints can be found in the Jews building a third Temple in Jerusalem before the Messiah comes to set up His kingdom. Once here, He will build the Temple, which is described in Ezekiel as over one mile large. This could not fit on the Temple Mount or even in Jerusalem. I believe Ezekiel states the fourth millennial Temple will be built north of Jerusalem.

On June 20, 1967, after Israel had captured the Temple Mount, *Time* magazine published the article, "Should the Temple Be Rebuilt?" The article stated:

"Assuming Israel keeps the Western Wall,
which is one of the few remaining ruins of

Judaism's second Temple, has the time now come for the erection of the third Temple? Such is Israel's euphoria today that some Jews see plausible theological grounds for discussing reconstruction. They base their argument on the contention that Israel has already entered its 'Messianic Era.' "

In 1948, they note, Israel's chief rabbi ruled that, with the establishment of the Jewish state and the ingathering of the exiles, "the age of redemption" had begun. Today, many of Israel's religious leaders are convinced that the Jews victory over the Arabs has taken Judaism well beyond that point. Historian Israel Eldad says:

"We are at the stage where David was when he liberated Jerusalem; from that time until the construction of the Temple of Solomon, only one generation passed, so will it be with us."

Israel has just passed the point of one generation, considered to be forty years, and their expectation that the Temple can be rebuilt is palatable. When I was in Jerusalem only a short time ago, I saw bumper stickers that said: "We Want Messiah Now." I saw posters displaying the Temple Mount with a rebuilt Temple superimposed over it.

The television show *60 Minutes* reported in March 1985, that rabbinical students in Jerusalem are now studying the reintroduction of the ancient Jewish rites of sacrifice on the Temple Mount. The show was called "One Step In Heaven." The show discussed Rabbi Shlomo Goren and the *yeshivas* studying the Levitical sacrifice system. While in Israel, I visited some of the *yeshivas*. In various secret places in the Old City I saw Orthodox students studying necessary details for Temple sacrifice and the rebuilding of the Temple. Models have been constructed of Temple vessels and utensils. A large model, painstakingly constructed to the smallest detail, has been created showing how the Temple needs to be rebuilt. Israel's control of the Temple Mount for the first time in two thousand years bring them to the point where they can speak practically of rebuilding the Temple.

In November 1981, Rabbi Goren in a *Newsweek* article stated that "the secret of the location of the Ark (of the Covenant) will be revealed just prior to the building of the third Temple." I have uncovered much evidence that the Ark of the Covenant still exists. The reason the tabernacle of the exodus was built was to house the Holy of Holies with the Ark of the Covenant. This is the same reason for Solomon's Temple, where the *shekinah* glory of God dwelt with Israel.

What happened to the Ark of the Covenant? Ethiopians claim that the Ark of the Covenant was taken to Ethiopia by the son of King Solomon and the Queen of Sheba. There is a picture of a mural from Ethiopia in my book, *Armageddon — Appointment with Destiny*, which describes the removal of the Ark.

This mural and others were done hundreds of years ago and are part of the national epoch of Ethiopia known as "The Glory Of the Kings." Translated, the mural says in part: "Solomon gives the Ark of the Covenant to his son, Menelik, which contained the Tablets of the Law of Moses." The next picture shows Menelik returning to Ethiopia with the Ark of the Covenant in his possession. He then gives it into the keeping of his mother, the Queen of Sheba. She later crowns him as the emperor of Ethiopia. The mural also mentions that the emperors claim direct descent from Menelik I, King Solomon of Judea, and the Queen of Sheba. The imperial coat of arms of Ethiopia, the monuments, and even jewelry of the country, even to this day have combined on them the Jewish seal of David and Christ on the cross.

In Acts 8, Phillip meets the Ethiopian eunuch. Many have wondered, why was this black Ethiopian, who was the treasurer to Queen Candace, returning home from Passover in Jerusalem? Why is he reading Isaiah 53? The answer is that this Ethiopian eunuch is descended from Menelik I, and Queen Candace, who was a Jewish queen of Ethiopia at this time. Though black, as a righteous Jew he attended Passover and was returning to Ethiopia. Phillip introduces him to Jesus Christ, the prophesied Messiah of Isaiah 53. Ethiopian records state that this eunuch was the first Ethiopian convert. The Ethiopian Coptic Church, one of the oldest in Christendom, was created based on Phillip's missionary effort.

In Ethiopia today, ten percent of the population are

black Jews known as Beta-Israel, the house of Israel. Non-Jewish Ethiopians call them *Falasha* Jews, or the exiles of Israel. They identify themselves in being from the house of Israel. Over half have become Christians, many in the last few hundred years and going back two thousand years to the Ethiopian eunuch's conversion. Because of government persecution, many Jews still in Ethiopia have been escaping to the Sudan and taken by secret airlift to Israel over the last five or six years. Unfortunately, the disclosure of this story several years ago led to its halt for a time, but many are still managing to flee Ethiopia and arrive in Israel. They have been accepted by Israel under the law of return as legitimate Jews.

Ethiopians claim to have the Ark of the Covenant in the city of Aksum, the ancient capitol of Ethiopia, in the northern province of Tigre. Recently, this area was captured by Tigre rebels and is under their control, not the control of the communist regime. Stephen Mengesha, crown prince of Ethiopia, now living in Canada, says that even the rebels, let alone the communist government, are afraid to touch the Ark of the Covenant. It is not on public display, but is held in a secret underground tunnel beneath the Church of Zion. It has been protected there for three thousand years by royal troops and Ethiopian Jews. Even though the monarchy is no longer in power, the Ethiopian priesthood continues its protection of the Ark, and I believe has been preserved by God all this time.

I realize other scholars believe that the Ark is still in

Israel, buried within tunnels under the Temple Mount. While that is a plausible theory, there is no biblical support for it. We won't know for sure where the Ark of the Covenant is until it is revealed in time for the rebuilding of the Temple, whether it is in Israel or in Ethiopia, as my research seems to indicate.

Zephaniah 3:9-10 talks about the generation in the last days when Hebrew will be rediscovered. This has happened since 1920 in Israel. God says: *"For then will I turn to the people a pure language, that they may all call upon the name of the Lord, to serve him with one consent. From beyond the rivers of Ethiopia my suppliants, even the daughter of my dispersed, shall bring mine offering"* (Zeph. 3:9-10). The question arises: What would Ethiopia have to bring? It could only be the Ark of the Covenant, taken three thousand years ago according to Ethiopian royal chronicles by Menelik I, son of Solomon. The replica of the Ark left in its place in the Holy of Holies would still be in Israel, if there is anything there at all.

God is calling out to the Ethiopians to bring the present back to Zion in Isaiah 18:1-3, 7. At the time of the end, verse six describes a great sacrifice of the enemy armies of God for the animals and birds. This is very similar to the battle prophesied in Ezekiel 38 and 39 in which the combined Russian-Arab forces are super-naturally defeated by God. Ezekiel 39:21-22 says: *"And I will set my glory among the heathen . . . So the house of Israel shall know that I am the Lord their God from that day and forward."* It is possible that God is saying in these verses that after the defeat of the Russian-Arab armies, He will allow the Ark of the Covenant to return to Israel for the rebuilding of the Temple. Isaiah 18:6 describes animals and birds feeding upon the Russian-Arab armies because there will be so many dead it will take seven months to bury them. Isaiah 18:7 seems in the same time sequence, after that great battle and sacrifice, as Ezekiel 39:21-22.

Only time will tell if the Ark is in Ethiopia or somewhere else. Jeremiah 3:15-16 I think clearly indicates that just before Jesus Christ returns and sets up His kingdom, the Ark of the Covenant will have been visited, talked about, and will once again be very important in Israel's worship activities. Once the Messiah comes, the Ark is no longer important because Jesus Christ Himself will be in Israel. All of this is only practical and possible if the Ark is recovered. Even at the time of Jeremiah, the Ark of the Covenant had already been lost for hundreds of years. The prophecy of Jeremiah implies that before Jesus Christ returns the Ark will have been revealed from its hiding place.

Ethiopia still claims to have the Ark of the Covenant in their possession. The Israeli secret service often asked Emperor Haile Selassie: "You have the Ark of the Covenant. Isn't it now time to bring the Ark back to Israel?" His answer was interesting. "In principle, I agree with you. But the timing is not right." He was waiting for a sign from God that they should return the Ark. I believe God will give that signal in the very near future.

How soon will Israel rebuild the Temple? The

Mishna, a commentary upon the Talmud and Torah, was prepared almost eight hundred years ago by Nemonbades, also known as Rambom, who also wrote *The Laws Of the Gods Chosen House*. He describes in this book how determined Israel is to rebuild the Temple. It says:

> *"The study of the Temple structure is of eternal significance. The Torah's six hundred thirteen laws and commands include the command to build the Temple. Until the Messiah comes, we can only fulfill that directive by studying its dimensions as recorded by our sages."*

Another rabbi, Rabbi Bachai writes:

> *"Know that the description of the sanctuary* [the Temple and its utensils] *and the research into its designs and dimensions fulfills a great command or* mitzvah, *even though the Temple itself is no longer standing."*

He goes on to state that by the merits of encircling and encompassing the walls of Jerusalem and studying the Temple, levels of the substructure of the Temple were revealed. In the Psalms it says God will return his *shekinah* glory to Zion's midsts, for this is our God forever. He will lead us eternally.

Even though this book was published only several

years ago, there is a comment in the book's beginning on the building of the Temple. The authors would frequently say to each other as they were preparing the text: "Work faster. At any moment, *Mashia* may come and rebuild the Temple. Who knows how the book may sell now!" This is an interesting comment from Orthodox Jews in the process of preparing these instructions for the rebuilding of the Temple. This book, along with several others, includes elaborate diagrams on rebuilding the Temple, with measurements and descriptions of the various vessels.

Chapter four of the *Mishna Torah* contains a commentary regarding the location of the original Temple. It says that the Ark of the Covenant was placed on a stone, part of the bedrock of Mount Moriah, in the western portion of the Holy of Holies. In Eyomah 53B the book continues to state that this was the foundation stone, known as the *Even Shetiyah*, and is now directly under the Dome of the Winds (also known by Arabs as the Dome of the Tablets) in a line directly opposite the Eastern Gate. This area is completely open, and the Temple could be rebuilt today on this site without disturbing the Dome of the Rock. The Dome of the Rock and the Temple would be well over one hundred and fifty feet apart.

Chapter six of the *Mishna Torah* confirms this, describing in precise detail to the exact cubic the dimensions of the walls, interior, and exterior of the Temple, including the positions of the gates. Five gates were placed in a straight line: the Eastern Gate, the gate to the chel shalel, the gate to the women's courtyard, the gate in the cantor, and the gate to the entrance hall. On the day for the sacrifice for the ashes of the red heifer, the priest could look directly from the Mount of Olives above the Eastern Gate (intentionally kept to a height of six cubics for this purpose), up the hill through all those gates into the veil of the Holy of Holies. Having stood on the very spot, this is only possible if the original Temple and the second Temple which Christ worshipped in were directly opposite the Eastern Gate, not where the Dome of the Rock is.

In Revelation 11, John says that only the Temple was to be measured. The Court of the Gentiles was not to be measured because it was given to the Gentiles, the unbelievers, for the latter part of the great tribulation. This, too, is consistent with the rebuilding of the Temple north of the Dome of the Rock. The dome would be allowed to exist, at least until Messiah comes.

These and many other reasons completely convince me that we are living in the last days. We are the first generation in history that with logic, as well as hope, can believe that we will live to see the coming of the Messiah, first for His church at the rapture, and then with His church in glory to launch the day in which the kingdom of this world truly becomes the kingdom of our Lord and Savior, Jesus Christ.

Chapter Six

Prophecies In the
First One Hundred Psalms

by J.R. Church

Why do I believe we live in the last days? Good question!

Though there are many prophetic passages in the Bible upon which to draw my conclusions, none are so specific or as detailed as the Psalms. When our Lord spoke of wars, famine, disease, and earthquakes, He was referring to this century. But theologians for the past twenty years have felt the same way.

William Miller chose 1843 for his proposed return of Christ. But he was not unique. There have been many others like him before and since. Interpretation of Bible prophecy of necessity enters the realm of speculation, for nobody knows the future. Nobody, that is, but God!

However, when we come to the Psalms, that is a different story. I have found the Psalms to be a diary of Israel's struggle to regain their promised land in this century. I don't mean just a reference here and there, but eighty-nine incredible years given in chronological order in each of the first eighty-nine psalms.

Now, everybody loves adventure. Who would not like to enter some dusty cave and find a treasure which would change the course of history? We watch with bated breath while some Indiana Jones crawls through snake-infested passages to find some long lost ark or discovers an ancient parchment which reveals the secret of the ages.

I propose to tell you that I have indeed found an ancient manuscript that tells (in cryptic language) the year by year account of the Jewish dispersion among the nations.

Israel has suffered long enough. The wandering Jew, at last, has been allowed to go home. God has decreed it — not in just one obscure passage, but in at least eighty-nine individual writings — written some three thousand years ago!

These ancient manuscripts were not just hidden away in some dusty cave through the centuries; God did a better job of preserving them. The great Creator had them copied and reproduced in practically every language of mankind. He put them in almost every household in almost every city of almost every nation, on almost every continent of the earth. What better way for God to preserve His prophecies of the last generation? When you think of it, that is a grand plan that only someone as great as God could acomplish.

Yet, they are there — in the Psalms — these prophecies giving a year-by-year account of Israel's restoration.

Furthermore, God had the Psalms placed as the nineteenth book of the Old Testament. Each psalm contains a reference, either explicit or implicit, of the Jewish struggle in each year of this century numbered according to each psalm. Book nineteen, chapter one opens the story of 1901. Book nineteen, chapter two captures the spirit of 1902. Book nineteen, chapter three reflects upon events in 1903 — and so forth through at least eighty-nine incredible psalms!

In Psalm 1 and 2, God sets the theme for the entire collection of the Psalms.

Psalm 1 expresses the theme of Israel's return under two prophetic symbols — the birth of the baby and the replanting of the tree. Though you may not realize that the opening passage, "Blessed is the man," refers to Israel, David did, in fact, choose Moses' last words to open his psalms. Moses put it this way: *"Happy art thou O Israel."* Cryptic? Yes! Without knowledge of the Jewish background of the two passages, a person would not recognize them as being the same statement. David wrote "Blessed is the man" and Moses called this man Israel!

In verse three, David wrote: *"He shall be like a tree, planted by the rivers of water. . . ."* One must be versed in the symbolism of the prophets to understand that the tree represents Israel. Furthermore, the word "planted" is actually the word "replanted," according to the original Hebrew language used in the passage.

Well, these are the two great themes of all prophecy — Israel is the man and Israel is the tree! We are thus introduced to the Psalms that tell the story of the return of the chosen people to their promised land at the end of the long winter of world history. That is the most important theme of the Psalms.

Psalm 2 continues this theme by referring to a time when the nations will "rage" or make war. The passage tells of a time when rulers will plot against the Lord and against Christ. The psalmist put it this way: *"Why do the heathen rage, and the people imagine a vain thing? The kings of the earth set themselves, and the rulers take counsel together, against the Lord, and against his anointed, saying, Let us break their bands asunder, and cast away their cords from us"* (Ps. 2:1-3).

Here is a world filled with politicians who conspire together to rid society of God — with all His commandments. Here is a United Nations where God is not welcome! — following on the heels of worldwide conflict — World War One and World War Two. But wait! Observe verses six through nine: *"Yet have I set my king upon my holy hill of Zion. I will declare the decree: the Lord hath said unto me, Thou art my Son; this day have I begotten thee. Ask of me, and I shall give thee the heathen for thine inheritance, and the uttermost parts of the earth for thy possession. Thou shalt break them with a rod of iron. . . ."*

Psalm 2 set the theme for this century — worldwide wars, nations uniting to rid society of God's laws, followed by the return of Christ to judge those nations and establish His glorious kingdom. The theme of each psalm (one and two) follow in conjunction with each other — the return of the Jews to their ancient homeland along with political maneuvers toward world government by politicians who hate God.

After setting the theme for the Psalms, David proceeded with a year-by-year account in each succeeding psalm. Let's pick a year, and then go to the psalm with the corresponding number to see if we can find some statement, some sentence, or some phrase that would seem to correspond with the events of that year.

Let's take the year 1917 when General Allenby and the British army surrounded the city of Jerusalem. The night before his impending invasion, Allenby, a Christian, prayed. He asked the Lord to allow him to take the city without destroying the holy places. The next morning, he sent hundreds of airplanes over the city. As they buzzed the Eastern Gate, one of the pilots dropped a note demanding surrender — signed by General Allenby.

Now, the word "Allah" in Arabic means God, and the word "beh" means son. The Turkish soldiers thought they were looking at a demand for surrender signed by Allah-beh, the son of God! In response, they hoisted the white flag, and surrendered the city without firing a single shot. The unusual event appeared to be a prophetic fulfillment of Isaiah 31:5 which says: *"As birds flying, so will the Lord of hosts defend Jerusalem; defending also he will deliver it; and passing over he will preserve it."*

Would you say Isaiah's passage was a prophecy? General Allenby did. He had the verse read to all his troops in Jerusalem. His superiors in London did. They sent him a telegram with that verse on it. Well, let's see what Psalm 17 might have to say about that event in 1917. Verse eight says: *"Keep me as the apple of the eye; hide me under the shadow of thy wings."*

Here is another cryptic reference to the wings of those British planes. How do we know that Psalm 17 was referring to British planes? Observe verse twelve: *"Like as a lion that is greedy of his prey. . . ."*

The lion is the symbol of Great Britain. But, of course, it must be just a coincidence that Psalm 17 appears to contain a cryptic reference of that which occurred in the seventeenth year of this century. Ah, but there is more!

Let's consider the highlights of the holocaust. 1932 saw the rise of Adolf Hitler in Germany. Thus began an ever increasing campaign against Jews. Psalm 32:3-4 seems to describe the attitude of the poor defenseless Jew: *"When I kept silence, my bones waxed old through my roaring all the day long. For day and night thy hand was heavy upon me: my moisture is turned into the drought of summer. . . ."*

The world just couldn't believe the reports coming out of Germany. Surely, the German people couldn't be so barbaric.

By March 15, 1933, the *Palestine Post*, a Jewish newspaper in Jerusalem, began to take note of Jewish persecution. The headline read, "Jews Flee Nazi's Reign of Terror." The article said: *"London hears of appalling persecutions and anti-Jewish measures."*

As the months progressed, Hitler developed his ideology of a German super race. He claimed Aryan supremacy — a pure bloodline to rule the world. And 1935 appears to be a picture of his continuing persecution against the Jews. Psalm 35 reflects the growing menace as the world approached the thirty-fifth year of this century. Verse one says: *"Plead my cause, O Lord, with them that strive with me: fight against them that fight against me."*

From the *Palestine Post* on October 28, 1935, came this headline: "Nazis Apply Nuremburg Laws Against the Jews in Germany." The article said:

> *"Jews in Germany may no longer partici-pate actively or passively in municipal elections, although they must continue to pay municipal taxes. . . .*
>
> *"The announcement explained that since the Jews are no longer citizens of the Reich, they are automatically deprived of their municipal citizenship rights."*

Then the plot thickens. By 1938 things were really getting bad in Germany, and Psalm 38:13-14, and 19 includes these words: *"But I, as a deaf man, heard not; and I was as a dumb man that openeth not his mouth. Thus I was as a man that heareth not, and in whose mouth are no reproofs. . . But mine enemies are lively, and they are strong: and they that hate me wrongfully are multiplied."*

Nazi crimes against the Jewish people were so fierce they were hard to believe. Most of the world turned a deaf ear to the atrocities. It seemed that few spoke out against Hitler. On November 11, 1838, however, the *Palestine Post* brandished this headline: "Nazi Hooligans Vent Wrath On the Jews Throughout Germany." Two days later the *Palestine Post* published this headline: "New Nazi Savagery Spells Doom Of Jewish Life In Germany." According to the report, Jews were hiding in the woods outside Berlin. There were reports of torture and murder.

By 1939 the situation was getting worse. Still, however, there was little outcry from around the world. Yet, in some incredible way, Psalm 39 seemed to capture the spirit of the year. Consider verses one through three: "*. . . I will keep my mouth with a bridle, while the wicked is before me. I was dumb with silence, I held my peace, even from good; and my sorrow was stirred. My heart was hot within me, while I was musing the fire burned. . . .*"

What fire? The crematoriums — the ovens of Auschwitz. This must surely be a cryptic prediction of those horrifying events that fell upon the Jews of Germany. By 1941 the situation worsened. We can read of it in Psalm 41:5 and 7: "*Mine enemies speak evil of me, When shall he die, and his name perish? . . . All that hate me whisper together against me: against me do they devise my hurt.*"

In the midst of the pressure, as Jews were herded into the concentration camps of Germany and Poland, the main question must have been: "When will this terrible atrocity be over?"

In 1942 the situation worsened. We can see it in Psalm 42. Consider verses three and nine: *"My tears have been my meat day and night, while they continually say unto me, Where is thy God? . . . I will say unto God my rock, Why hast thou forgotten me? why go I mourning because of the oppression of the enemy?"*

By 1943 the German nation and their diabolical leader, Hitler, had launched a terrible holocaust the Jews. Before it was over, six million Jews were slaughtered and their bodies burned in the awful ovens of the concentration camps. Psalm 43:1: *"Judge me, O God, and plead my cause against an ungodly nation: O deliver me from the deceitful and unjust man."*

I believe the passage is a cryptic reference to Germany and Hitler. At first I felt we could only speculate. Yet, the comparison was uncanny. Now I am convinced. What happened in 1944? We can read of it in Psalm 44:9, 11, 14, 22-23: *"But thou hast cast off, and put us to shame. . . . Thou hast given us like sheep appointed for meat; and hast scattered us among the heathen. . . . Thou makest us a byword among the heathen. . . . Yea, for thy sake are we killed all the day long; we are counted as sheep for the slaughter. Awake, why sleepest thou, O Lord? arise, cast us not off for ever."*

What an incredible description of Hitler's holocaust! And, you know, it seemed that the Lord did awaken that year and hear the cry of the distraught Jewish people, for in the next psalm, the war was turned against the enemies of God's chosen people. *"Gird thy sword upon thy thigh, O most mighty, with thy glory and thy majesty. And in thy majesty ride prosperously because of truth and meekness and righteousness; and thy right hand shall teach thee terrible things. Thine arrows are sharp in the heart of the king's enemies; whereby the people fall under thee"* (Ps. 45:3-5).

Yes, 1945 saw the suicide of Adolf Hitler and the devastation of the German army. However, six million Jews were dead — a third of the world's Jewish population. But, wait a minute. All was not lost, for a promise appears in Psalm 45:16-17: *"Instead of thy fathers shall be thy children, whom thou mayest make princes in all the earth. I will make thy name to be remembered in all generations. . . ."*

Though a generation of German Jews had been brutally butchered, their children were to return to their ancient homeland, establish a government, be made princes in all the earth, and, according to the psalm, make the world to remember in all generations those who suffered the holocaust.

Psalm 46 reflects upon the devastation of World War Two. Verse eight says, *"Come, behold the works of the Lord, what desolations he hath made in the earth."*

Take a look at Berlin! "What desolations he hath made in the earth." Take a look at London! "What desolations he hath made in the earth." Take a look at Hiroshima! "What desolations he hath made in the earth." Verse nine says, *"He maketh wars to cease unto the end of the earth. . . ."*

"He maketh wars to cease" wrote the psalmist, and

that well characterizes the conclusions of worldwide war. From the Atlantic to the Pacific, "He maketh wars to cease." From Germany to Japan, "He maketh wars to cease." From one end of the earth to the other, "He maketh wars to cease."

According to the *New York Times* on May 2, 1945, Adolf Hitler committed suicide, and within the week the war in Europe was ended. On August 7, 1945, the first atomic bomb was dropped on Japan. Two days later another bomb was loosed on Nagasaki, and by August 15, 1945, Japan surrendered, thus ending World War Two. For the first time (in oh, so long) New Years Day of 1946 witnessed a world at peace. What an incredible statement to be found in Psalm 46: *"He maketh wars to cease. . . ."*

From that point the Jewish people across Europe set out to return to Palestine. The thrust of the year was: "Let's go home." Psalm 46:4-6 says: *"There is a river, the streams whereof shall make glad the city of God, the holy place of the tabernacles of the most High. God is in the midst of her; she shall not be moved: God shall help her, and that right early. The heathen raged, the kingdoms were moved. . . ."*

There's that same statement which set the theme of the Psalms in Psalm 2: *"Why do the heathen rage?"* Psalm 46:6 says: *"The heathen raged!"*

And you know, 1947 witnessed a struggle for Israel's ancient inheritance. The year appears to be described in Psalm 47:4: *"He shall choose our inheritance for us, the excellency of Jacob whom he loved. . . ."*

What about 1948? That was the year for the replanting of the tree and the birth of the baby; the nation of Israel was born. Psalm 48:1-2 says: *"Great is the Lord, and greatly to be praised in the city of our God, in the mountain of his holiness. Beautiful for situation, the joy of the whole earth, is mount Zion, on the sides of the north, the city of the great King."*

The word "situation" is a cryptic key. In the original Hebrew language, it is the word *noph*. It means "a tree" — not just a branch or twig, but a huge tree replanted in Jerusalem!

On May 14, 1948, the flag of the Israeli nation was hoisted over the land for the first time in one thousand eight hundred thirteen years. Throughout the Jewish world there was rejoicing and gladness. The emotion of the occasion was electric among the Jews.

The Gentile world, however, did not view the rebirth of the state of Israel with the same enthusiasm — especially the British, for they had been driven out of the land. It was an awesome and troubling scene as the British witnessed those birthpangs of travail. Psalm 48:4-7 describes those events which occurred in the forty-eighth year of this century with uncanny detail: *"For, lo, the kings were assembled, they passed by together. They saw it, and so they marvelled; they were troubled, and hasted away. Fear took hold upon them there, and pain, as of a woman in travail. Thou breakest the ships of Tarshish. . . . "*

"The ships of Tarshish," said the psalmist. It is an unbelievably accurate description of the British — those men of Tarshish — as they boarded their ships in the harbor at Haifa and pushed off into the Mediterranean. They had seen the incredible "woman in travail." Yes, Psalm 48 presents an uncanny description of those events fulfilled in 1948.

Psalm 49:1-4 continues this special message to what Psalm 48 described as the "generation following." "*Hear this, all ye people; give ear, all ye inhabitants of the world: Both low and high, rich and poor, together. My mouth shall speak of wisdom; and the meditation of my heart shall be of understanding. I will incline mine ear to a parable: I will open my dark saying. . . .*"

Please note: With the birth of the state of Israel, God has declared a special message to the generation following the birth of Israel. He declared that He will open those dark sayings so that His people might begin to understand. This is the same kind of promise given in Daniel 12:4, when God said: "*. . . shut up the words, and seal the book, even to the time of the end . . . knowledge shall be increased.*"

Dear friend, we live in that special generation chosen to understand the prophecies. Furthermore, the Lord said in Psalm 49:4: "*I will incline mine ear to a parable. . . .*"

Which parable? It could be the one spoken by Jesus when He said: "*Now learn a parable of the fig tree; When his branch is yet tender, and putteth forth leaves, ye know that summer is nigh: So likewise ye, when ye shall see all these things, know that it is near, even at the doors. Verily I say unto you, This generation shall not pass, till all these things be fulfilled"* (Matt. 24:32-34).

That is the parable, and this is the generation. How incredible it is that the promise is made in Psalm 49 — which appears to represent that first year following the rebirth of the state of Israel and the budding of the fig tree. Remember, that was the subject introduced in Psalm 1:3: *". . . he shall be like a tree planted by the rivers of water, that bringeth forth his fruit in his season. . . ."*

The budding of the fig tree! Now we can begin to understand the prophecies. God appears to be lifting the proverbial veil from the eyes of his people.

Prophecies which were heretofore not understood are beginning to make sense. And the return of the Jewish people to their ancient land represents the key to the understanding of prophecy.

Is it any wonder, then, that I believe we live in the last days?

Though the Psalms represent the heartbeat of an ancient Jewish culture, they also have within them the cryptic language of a prophet. The skeptic may ask: Do the Psalms declare a prophetic design? Was David, the sweet singer of Israel, a prophet as well?

To the skeptic, I would return this question: Would God have allowed David and others to write so many of the Psalms without including in them His great plan of the ages? Furthermore, since prophecy was so important in the religious thinking of early Judaism, would not God also have provided prophecies in their music?

I have found that the Psalms were compiled in

chronological order — perhaps even numerical order — according to the events predicted for this century. We have considered a sampling of the first forty-nine psalms which relate to those events affecting the Jewish people in the first forty-nine years of this century. For example, Psalm 17 contains certain statements which refer to events occurring in 1917 — the year General Allenby took the city of Jerusalem from the Turkish government.

Furthermore, we considered a number of passages from Psalm 32-45 which contain cryptic descriptions of the holocaust which befell the Jewish people during the years from 1932 through 1945. We also took note of the following Psalms which describe the rebirth of the state of Israel. The descriptions contained in Psalm 48 have an uncanny parallel to certain events surrounding the 1948 birth of Israel. Psalm 48:6 says: *"Fear took hold upon them there, and pain, as of a woman in travail."*

Now the question: If the first forty-eight Psalms contain cryptic descriptons of those events which occurred in the first forty-eight years of this century, do the rest of the Psalms contain similar descriptions of those events which have occurred since 1948 to the present day? My answer is, YES! Furthermore, Psalms 90 through 100 contain the prophetic Song of Moses, which describe the events of the tribulation period — the rise of the Antichrist, the abomination of desolation, the battle of Armageddon, and the glorious coming of Christ to judge the nations and establish His millennial kingdom!

In Revelation 15, we are told that the saints in

Heaven sing this Song of Moses during the tribulation period at the point when seven angels are about to pour out the vials of God's wrath upon the earth. That's how important and prophetic this Song of Moses is to the fulfillment of prophecy. I cannot tell you that the events will be fulfilled in the years numbered according to those psalms. But, I can tell you that the prophetic events will occur. I cannot tell you when; I do not know the future. I can only relate to the first eighty-nine psalms. They refer to the past and the present.

However, because of the prophetic nature of the first eighty-nine psalms, I am convinced that we live in the last generation.

Let us review Psalm 48 as a prophetic description of 1948 and the birth of the nation of Israel. Let us take note that in verse thirteen, the psalmist wrote that we should mark the event and tell it to the generation following: *"Mark ye well her bulwarks, consider her palaces; that ye may tell it to the generation following."*

The term "generation following" is most interesting. The Hebrew word translated following is *acharon*. It means "last." The psalmist says to tell it to the **last** generation!

This marks the beginning of a special generation like the one referred to by Jesus in Matthew 24:34 when He said: *". . . This generation shall not pass, till all these things be fulfilled."*

Now, let us consider the psalms which follow and see if we can find some statement which describes an important event for that year in the life of the Jewish people. For example, in Psalm 50:5 the psalmist wrote: *"Gather my saints together unto me. . . ."*

That appears to be a prophetic description of the Law of Return passed by the Israeli parliament on July 6, 1950. The Law of Return was passed unanimously by the Knesset allowing any Jew in the world to immigrate to Israel. David Ben Gurion described it as a "charter" to the Jews of the world that they might come home to Israel. *"Gather my saints together unto me. . . ."*

The following psalms appear to contain the same general theme. Psalm 53:6 continues: *". . . When God bringeth back the captivity of his people, Jacob shall rejoice, and Israel shall be glad."*

Psalm 51 gives the description of a sinful people who are seeking the forgiveness of God. The psalm was written by David after his sin with Bathsheba. According to C.I. Scofield, however, the chapter has a dispensational reference. He said: *"It will be the pathway of returning Israel."*

Scofield wrote that in 1909, long before the return of the Jew to his land. Yet it is true. God's chosen people are returning both to their promised land — and eventually to their Messiah. The psalm, of course, contains more than could be fulfilled completely in 1951, but its description reveals the heartbeat of the Jewish people during those early days. It describes that which has developed over the years and will continue to progress until the Messiah comes. Psalm 51:1 says: *"Have mercy upon me, O God, according to thy lovingkindness: according unto the multitude of thy tender mercies blot out my transgressions."*

David Ben Gurion was the first prime minister of Israel, but on December 8, 1953, Ben Gurion retired. He left the hectic world of politics and moved to a little ranch in the Negev Desert where he wanted to spend the rest of his life as a sheep farmer. He just wanted to get away from it all. But alas, circumstances would not allow, for in 1955 he returned to the government as Minister of Defense. Psalm 55 appears to describe Ben Gurion's return in 1955. Consider verses six and seven: *"And I said, Oh that I had wings like a dove! for then would I fly away, and be at rest. Lo, then would I wander far off, and remain in the wilderness. . . ."*

But he could not remain in the wilderness, for he was needed in the position of Minister of Defense. Why? Verse three says, *"Because of the voice of the enemy, because of the oppression of the wicked. . . ."*

Obvserve verses nine through eleven: *". . . for I have seen violence and strife in the city. Day and night they go about it upon the walls thereof: mischief also and sorrow are in the midst of it. Wickedness is in the midst thereof: deceit and guile depart not from her streets."*

On February 1, 1961, Ben Gurion tried again to resign but without success, for his government and his people still needed him. Psalm 61:6 says: *"Thou wilt prolong the king's life. . . ."*

By June 17, 1963, however, Ben Gurion had determined to retire. He resigned for the last time and meant it. Perhaps that's why the psalmist concluded Psalm 63 with these words in verse eleven: *"But the king shall rejoice in God. . . ."*

David Ben Gurion died on November 1, 1973. Perhaps that is a reference of the passage in Psalm 73:24 and 26: *"Thou shalt guide me with thy counsel, and afterward receive me to glory. . . . My flesh and my heart faileth. . . ."*

Through the years since 1948 there has been a continual thorn in the side of Israel. It has taken the form of sporadic fighting between the Arabs and the Jews. For example, on March 16, 1954, eleven bus passengers were massacred by Arabs on a road near Beersheba. Perhaps that's what the psalmist had reference to in Psalm 54:3 when he wrote: *"For strangers are risen up against me. . . ."*

On April 6, 1956, the Egyptian army created a disturbance in the Gaza Strip. Six Israelis were wounded, and Egypt suffered one hundred and forty casualties. In the months that followed, however, it was to explode into a full-scale war. Could that be what the psalmist described in Psalm 56:1-2? *"Be merciful unto me, O God: for man would swallow me up; he fighting daily oppresseth me. Mine enemies would daily swallow me up: for they be many that fight against me. . . ."*

On October 30, a full-scale war erupted. The headline in the *Jerusalem Post* read: "Army Attacks Bases In Heart Of Sinai." The next day, the British and the French bombed Cairo. On November 2, Egypt's Sinai army was in full flight, and Israeli forces sealed off the Gaza Strip. By November 4, the battle in the Sinai was over. Israel was the clear victor. All of this occurred in 1956, and in Psalm 56 we have what appears to be a cryptic description. Consider verses seven through nine: *"Shall they escape by iniquity? in thine anger cast down the people, O God. Thou tellest my wanderings: put thou my tears into thy bottle: are they not in thy book? When I cry unto thee, then shall mine enemies turn back: this I know; for God is for me."*

Verse twelve says, *"Thy vows are upon me. . . ."* Yes, the 1956 war over the Gaza Strip appears to be the subject of Psalm 56.

In 1961, the Israeli nation became thirteen years old. That was the year Israel was recognized as a full-fledged developed nation by the U.N. General Assembly. It was declared to be their national Bar Mitzvah. That just happens to be the subject of Psalm 61:5: *"For thou, O God, hast heard my vows: thou hast given me the heritage of those that fear thy name."*

In 1964 Yasser Arafat organized the Palestinian Liberation Organization. From that day forward the PLO has been a thorn in the side of Israel. The year was 1964, and in Psalm 64:2-5 we can find these words: *"Hide me from the secret counsel of the wicked; from the insurrection of the workers of iniquity: Who whet their tongue like a sword, and bend their bows to shoot their arrows, even bitter words: That they may shoot in secret at the perfect: suddenly do they shoot at him, and fear not. They encourage themselves in an evil matter. . . ."*

In 1966 Egypt began beating the war drums again. The resulting conflicts between Israel and Egypt led to two major wars — the Six-Day War of 1967 and the

Yom Kippur War of 1973. In 1977 Anwar Sadat came before the Israeli Knesset in Jerusalem with his offer of peace. Menachem Begin and Anwar Sadat signed the resulting peace treaty on the White House lawn in 1979. The Arab world was furious. As a result, Anwar Sadat was assassinated on October 2, 1981. Now please note, from Psalm 66 to Psalm 81 the Israeli people are reminded over and over again of their original exodus out of Egypt — uncanny, but true. Psalm 66:6 says: *"He turned the sea into dry land: they went through the flood on foot: there did we rejoice in him."*

Psalm 68:7 says: *"O God, when thou wentest forth before thy people, when thou didst march through the wilderness. . . ."*

Psalm 74:13 says: *"Thou didst divide the sea by thy strength. . . ."*

Psalm 77:5 says: *"I have considered the days of old, the years of ancient times."*

Consider Psalm 78:12-13: *"Marvellous things did he in the sight of their fathers, in the land of Egypt. . . . He divided the sea, and caused them to pass through; and he made the waters to stand as an heap."*

Observe Psalm 80:8, 15-16: *"Thou hast brought a vine out of Egypt. . . . And the vineyard which thy right hand hath planted, and the branch that thou madest strong for thyself. It is burned with fire, it is cut down. . . ."*

Psalm 81:10 says: *"I am the Lord thy God, which brought thee out of the land of Egypt. . . ."*

These references seemed to be placed strategically

in the light of Israel's relationship with Egypt. It seems that God is reminding the Israeli people that this generation can be likened to the generation of the exodus when Moses led the children of Israel out of Egypt. In fact, the exodus out of Europe in 1947 was so much like the exodus out of Egypt that even Psalm 47 makes a reference to it.

Psalm 67 seems to reflect upon the results of the war of 1967. In the famous Six-Day War the city of Jerusalem was reunited under Jewish control for the first time in nearly two thousand years. Jews from around the world rejoiced in that most historic and important occasion. Consider Psalm 67:4-5: *"O let the nations be glad and sing for joy: for thou shalt judge the people righteously, and govern the nations upon earth. Selah Let the people praise thee, O God; let all the people praise thee."*

The beginning verses of Psalm 68 seem to reflect upon the military aspects of war: *"Let God arise, let his enemies be scattered: let them also that hate him flee before him. As smoke is driven away, so drive them away . . ."* (Ps. 68:1-2).

Psalm 73 seems to relate to the Yom Kippur War. Israel was caught off guard in the surprise attack. In those first few days it looked as if Israel would not survive. Psalm 73:2 says: *"But as for me, my feet were almost gone; my steps had well nigh slipped."*

Verse fourteen says, *"For all the day long have I been plagued, and chastened every morning."*

Israel was able to turn the war, however, and win a

decisive victory. Yes, there was victory, but there was no peace. No Arab nation was willing to recognize the sovereignty of the state of Israel — until 1977, when Anwar Sadat made his famous offer of peace. Negotiations began immediately and continued throughout the following year of 1978. They were long and difficult. It seemed at times that there would be no peace. It was such an important year in Israel's relationship with Egypt that Psalm 78 spent a full seventy-two verses on the subject. In fact, the psalmist started out by saying in verses one and two, *"Give ear, O my people, to my law: incline your ears to the words of my mouth. I will open my mouth in a parable: I will utter dark sayings of old."*

The peace treaty between Israel and Egypt represented the fulfillment of Bible prophecy, and the psalmist indicated the importance of those "dark sayings of old."

In Psalm 80 we seem to have a description of that special man who was to bring the two nations to the peace table. In the psalm, Anwar Sadat appears to be represented through the parable of a vine. Verse eight says, *"Thou hast brought a vine out of Egypt. . . ."*

Could that be a prophetic reference to Anwar Sadat, who came to Jerusalem with his offer of peace? Could it be a picture of that man whose life was cut short because he signed a peace treaty with the Jews? Please note what happened to the vine in verses fifteen and sixteen, *"And the vineyard which thy right hand hath planted, and the branch that thou madest strong for thyself. It is burned with fire, it is cut down. . . ."*

What incredible descriptions are given! What

incredible implications are made concerning Israel's relationship with Egypt from Psalm 66 through Psalm 81.

On September 29, 1981, the Jewish people celebrated Rosh Hashanah (New Years Day) for the Jewish year 5742. It is interesting to note that many dates were set for the rapture that year — perhaps more than any other year in history — up until 1988. However, though 1981 did not represent the beginning of the tribulation period, Rosh Hashanah did seem to mark a milestone in prophetic fulfillment. Perhaps that is why we can read in Psalm 81:3: *"Blow up the trumpet in the new moon, in the time appointed, on our solemn feast day."*

Yes, the Feast of Trumpets was important enough to be noted in what appears to be its corresponding psalm.

On June 6, 1982, the Israeli army launched "Operation Peace for Galilee." They moved into Lebanon to disperse the PLO. They just couldn't take it any more. Arafat's army had continually pressured the Israeli nation with acts of terrorism. After a renewed round of Ketusha rockets, the Jewish people decided they had had enough. Perhaps that is why we read in Psalm 82:2-4: *"How long will ye judge unjustly, and accept the persons of the wicked? Selah. Defend the poor and fatherless: do justice to the afflicted and needy. Deliver the poor and needy: rid them out of the hand of the wicked."*

That brings us to 1983. Arafat met with Jordan's King Hussein. He tried to rally support for his dispersed

PLO. Perhaps that is why we read in Psalm 83:2-5: *"For, lo, thine enemies make a tumult: and they that hate thee have lifted up the head. They have taken crafty counsel against thy people, and consulted against thy hidden ones. They have said, Come, and let us cut them off from being a nation; that the name of Israel may be no more in remembrance. For they have consulted together with one consent: they are confederate against thee."*

Who is this enemy described in these verses? Can we be sure that it is the same enemy of Israel which has conspired over the past several months? As a matter of fact, the enemy is named in verses six through eight: *"The tabernacles of Edom, and the Ishmaelites; of Moab, and the Hagarenes; Gebal, and Ammon, and Amalek; the Philistines with the inhabitants of Tyre; Assur also is joined with them: they have holpen the children of Lot. . . ."*

Please note, the country of Jordan is described by the ancient tribes listed in these verses — Edom, Moab, and Ammon. Furthermore, the Philistines or Palestinians are listed along with the inhabitants of Tyre in Lebanon! Incredible, but there it is. It describes in the language of three thousand years ago, the enemies of Israel in 1983.

Psalm 84 describes the beginning of Jewish efforts to regain the Temple Mount — which continues to this very day.

Psalm 85 contains a reference to the rescue of the black Jews from Ethiopia.

Psalm 86 again turns toward the restoration of Temple worship and may also contain a reference to the

Ark of the Covenant.

Psalm 87 relates to MYSTERY BABYLON, destined to rise to power during the tribulation period.

Psalm 88 describes the Palestinian unrest in the occupied territories. It is a problem for which there is no solution.

And Psalm 89 concludes this dramatic portion of the Psalms which began in Psalm 73. The psalmist directs us toward Jewish efforts to regain the Temple Mount and establish Temple worship. Such a worship will be necessary during the tribulation so that the Antichrist can commit the abomination of desolation.

The details of this portion of the Psalms are so numerous, I can only suggest that you read the rest of the story in my book, *Hidden Prophecies in the Psalms*.

By now I think you can see why I am convinced that we live in the last days!

Chapter Seven

Israel —
The Great Indicator

by Rob Lindsted

Haven't people always said that we are living in the last days? What makes today so different?

It is important for us to look at the Bible and see how God is fulfilling the words written by the ancient prophets, especially concerning the subject of Israel. I believe Israel is one of the greatest indicators that we are living in the last days.

Titus 2:13 says that we are to be *"Looking for that blessed hope, and the glorious appearing of the great God and our Saviour Jesus Christ."* I know this command was given some nineteen hundred years ago, but never has it been more true than today. We ought to be looking for the return of Jesus Christ at any moment. I believe the reason we can say we are living in the last days is because as we go to the Bible, especially to the writings of the prophet Ezekiel, which were written some twenty-five hundred years ago. We begin to see the great fulfillment that God has allowed those of us alive today to witness with our very own eyes.

Ezekiel 36:24 is a remarkable verse. In this verse, God says through the prophet Ezekiel that before Christ comes to set up a millennial kingdom, a thousand-year rule and reign, certain conditions will exist.

Before this thousand-year period begins, however, there will be a time of trouble called the tribulation. The details of this tribulation are discussed in Revelation chapters six through nineteen. The Bible is very clear: Before the tribulation ever begins Christ will come and catch away those who are true believers in Jesus Christ. This is called the rapture, and while the word "rapture" is not mentioned in the Bible, the catching away certainly is, as we read in 1 Thessalonians 4 and 1 Corinthians 15.

As we look at the nation of Israel, it is an indication that God is in the process of bringing about the thousand years of rule and reign by Christ.

Now, let's look at some of the indicators the prophet Ezekiel said would take place before the millennial kingdom would ever come. In Ezekiel 36:24 it says: *"For I will take you from among the heathen, and gather you out of all countries, and will bring you into your own land."* Here is one of the predictions made by God through the prophet Ezekiel. He said: *"When Israel has been scattered and regathered into their own land, you know you are living in the last days."* Forty-five years ago, people could not have said this. But today we can, for we have witnessed in a dramatic way the return of the nation of Israel.

As we look at Satan's attack upon the nation of Israel and upon the Jewish people, it is very clear that he is aware that God is in the process of fulfilling His Word. For example, when God wanted to send a deliverer to Israel through the person of Moses, Pharaoh tried to wipe out all the male children of Israel. He wanted to keep Israel as slaves in Egypt. And then we come to the time of the birth of Christ. Again, we remember that there was a king who wanted to wipe out all the Jewish boys, hoping to stop the Messiah from ever coming. As we come to the 1940s, Hitler was determined to wipe out the Jewish race. Why? Because he understood that before God would come and set up a millennial kingdom, the nation of Israel would have to be reborn, would have to come back into their own land, and if he could wipe out the Jewish people, he could stop God's plan.

My dear friend, it didn't work, did it? Hitler failed. And not only did the annihilation of Israel not take place as Hitler planned, although six million-plus Jews were murdered, but we know that at the end of that time period the Jews were fueled more than ever to have their own homeland. Every time Satan tried to stop God's plan, we see that God fulfilled it in a great and mighty way.

Ezekiel 36:24 is a result of God saying: "I am more powerful than Satan. My plan is in effect and it will come to pass." In 70 A.D. the nation of Israel was scattered. They were spread out into all the world. And yet some eighteen hundred years later, God called them back after great persecution and they are at home in their own land. We have witnessed a great miracle. I think Israel is a great indicator that we are living in the last days. God is fulfilling His promise in an amazing way.

People ask why Ezekiel 36 couldn't be fulfilled as the children of Israel came back from some of the captivities. Well, there is a very good reason why it could not be fulfilled then. Luke 21:24 says: *"And they shall fall by the edge of the sword, and shall be led away captive into all nations: and Jerusalem shall be trodden down of the Gentiles, until the times of the Gentiles be fulfilled."* Christ repeats the prophecy of Ezekiel. He says Israel will come back into their own land after they have been trodden down by the Gentiles.

But He also says that Jerusalem shall be trodden down. It is interesting that many nations have held Jerusalem captive since 70 A.D. when Jerusalem was taken by the Romans under General Titus. And yet, God said there will be a day when Gentiles will no longer control Jerusalem. We have seen that day. In the last twenty-two years Jerusalem has changed hands. It is now in the hands of the Jews again, exactly as Christ said and as the prophet Ezekiel implied.

But the Bible didn't stop there. Ezekiel 36:35 says: *"And they shall say, This land that was desolate is become like the garden of Eden. . . ."* Not only will Israel be back in their own land with Jerusalem under their control, but the land that was a desert will be like the garden of Eden. If you were to travel to Israel today, you would find a land that was a desert just five or six years ago, today is a thriving farming community.

In the September 1987 issue of *Saturday Evening Post*, there is an article which documents Israel's food from the desert. The article begins by saying that it had been projected that the desert would be able to feed only half a million people. In other words, the entire nation of Israel could only supply food for half a million people. But today over half a million people are living right in the very area that was called uninhabitable just a few years ago.

Furthermore, in addition to half a million people living in that area, there are two hundred and fifty thriving farming communities, not just farms, but whole farming settlements. And the amazing thing about these farming settlements is that they are actually using salt water, water twenty times saltier than drinking water, to water their plants in the desert. And these plants are producing incredible yields. For example, the article mentions a man who is harvesting his third crop of the season of melons, tomatoes, eggplants, peppers, dates, zucchinis, and avocadoes. These are shipped to Europe, arriving weeks and months ahead of the other produce, where premium prices are given. They are growing as much as sixty tons of food per acre. That's four to six times what a farmer can grow in the United States. In other words, what we are seeing before our very eyes is the desert turn into a garden, exactly as the Bible says.

Another article talks about the fact that over four hundred species of flowers and trees are now grown in Israel. They are shipped several times a year to markets in Germany, England, France, and Holland. This is incredible. We think of Holland in terms of flowers, and yet Israel imports flowers to Holland.

Here's another article I think you will be interested in which proves that the desert of a few years ago is now a garden. This article states that Israel is now producing peaches in a very unique way. They plant peaches in buckets and put them into cold storage. They then bring them out of cold storage and place them in the frost-free Jordan Valley. Again, we find the area that was once desert is now an orchard or garden, exactly as the Bible predicted.

We can say we are living in the last days because Israel is such a great fulfillment of Bible prophecy. The land has been restored to its rightful owner; Jerusalem has come back under Jewish control; and, the desert has changed into a garden.

The Bible also says that in the last days the waste, desolate cities would become fortified and inhabited. Again, if you were to travel to Israel today, you would find a number of cities that have been rebuilt. The Bible actually said that certain cities of the Philistines would be destroyed and rebuilt. Among those today you can find the cities of Ashkelon and Ashdod. These cities were once destroyed exactly as the Bible predicted in the book of Zephaniah, but today they are inhabited. As a matter of fact, one of them has a population of forty thousand and is Israel's largest deep-water seaport.

I marvel as I look at these passages. In Amos 9 we find some great verses that are being fulfilled today.

Verse thirteen says, *"Behold, the days come, saith the Lord, that the plowman shall overtake the reaper, and the treader of grapes him that soweth seed. . . ."* In other words, in the same field there will be both people planting and reaping. That's how quickly the crops will be coming out of the ground. This is being fulfilled in Israel today.

It also says in verse fourteen, *"And I will bring again the captivity of my people of Israel, and they shall build the waste cities, and inhabit them; and they shall plant vineyards, and drink the wine thereof; they shall also make gardens, and eat the fruit of them."* That is exactly what is taking place. Right where cities are being rebuilt, the gardens are being planted.

We are seeing great fulfillments of the Bible. We are seeing it through Israel, because God said that before He ever sets up a millennial kingdom there will be a tribulation. And before the tribulation comes, there will be a catching out of the church. One of the greatest indicators that we are living in the last days is seeing how God is fulfilling His Word through the ancient prophecies according to the nation of Israel.

The Bible says in Isaiah 27:6 that *". . . Israel shall blossom and bud, and fill the face of the world with fruit."* Israel is now exporting food throughout Europe and the rest of the world. God is fulfilling His Word in a great way.

In Ezekiel 37:1-10, we have a great story. It is the story of how God promised Ezekiel he would be able to recognize the last days. I believe we are living in those days.

He would be able to recognize them in a very special way. God illustrated this to Ezekiel by saying: "Go to a graveyard. As you walk through this open valley, what do you see?" And the response was: "I see bones — bones that are dry and dead." Because these bones were dry and dead, it was clear that there had been no life in them for a very long time. These bones that are Israel were dead and scattered throughout all the world. But as God's Word came to life, these bones came to life. He said: "Speak my living word unto them." And as Ezekiel spoke the living word unto them, the bones began to shake, rattle and move. The foot bones all fit together and they joined to the ankle bones, and the leg bones, and so on, and pretty soon skeletons stood erect there in the graveyard. Then the Bible says in verses six and seven that flesh came on them. And then God put breath in them. Finally it is summarized: *"So I prophesied as he commanded me, and the breath came into them, and they lived, and stood up upon their feet, an exceeding great army"* (Ezek. 37:10).

This is an amazing story, not because there is a famous song about it, but because it makes a prediction that only God could fulfill. The Bible says the last days will be very clear: Israel will be back in their land; Jerusalem will be under Jewish control; the desert will bloom; cities will be rebuilt; and, Israel will supply food throughout the entire world.

And He said it will also be clear because Israel will be an exceedingly great army. If you look at the history of Israel from the days of Saul, the great King Solomon, or any other king, you will find that Israel was never a great military power — until now. Today, Israel has won the respect of the world because they really are a great military power. In the last forty years Israel has won five national battles. I believe that today Russia is afraid to attack Israel because of Israel's great ability to respond in such an emergency. The Bible says it will be clear the last days have come, because Israel will be a great army. At no time in the entire history of Israel could anyone claim Israel was a great army. But today we can.

It is interesting to see the headlines we find in our newspapers today. These headlines show how clearly the world recognizes the military ability of Israel. In the *Toronto Star*, there is an article in which Russia says to Israel: "You shouldn't build the Jericho II missile." They warn that because Israel has the Jericho II missile, they are just one missile away from being able to wipe out the entire population center of Egypt. Fifty percent of the population would be wiped out with one missile, as it would destroy the dam. It quotes Moscow Radio warning Israel not to continue the development of the Jericho II missile. They claim this is really an American-inspired threat to destroy Soviet strategic centers. But the real truth is that the Soviet authorities admit they are worried about Israel's technological ability as developed in missiles and other weapons. This is great, huge Russia afraid of little Israel. Israel is only forty years old and they are a small nation. But the Bible says that in the last days they would be a great military power. Today they strike fear even in the heart of their archenemy, Russia.

What I see as the result of peace between Iran and Iraq is Israel having to prepare for war with them. You see, as so-called peace came into Iraq and Iran, the Soviet troops were free to build up around Israel. There were one hundred and fifteen thousand troops in Afghanistan. Where did they go? Many of them centered into Lebanon and Syria to build up the forces of the Soviet Union there.

In an Associated Press article, Israel's military chief of staff says his troops have already held drills to prepare for possible warfare with airbombings after the Iran-Iraq war ended. He said we have to also take Syria into account. He says that Iraq has sent ground forces to fight Israel in three of the five wars that the Jewish state has fought since 1948. They realize that as peace comes to these other countries, it simply allows Russia, as well as other Arab countries, to concentrate on Israel. He also predicts that any future war between Israel and Syria "will be much more costly, more bloody, than it's ever been in the past." He mentions that there is a great buildup in Damascus, an improvement in quality and quantity of military equipment. All of this, including chemical warheads for surface-to-surface missiles, comes directly from Russia. They've increased the number of tanks by some thirty-three hundred just recently. Syria has also doubled the number of attack aircraft in their arsenal. This is exactly what the Bible says. In Ezekiel 38 and 39 it says that Syria, under the buildup of Russia, will pose a great threat to Israel.

We are seeing the Bible fulfilled, because we are living in the last days. How do we know? Israel is a great indicator that the plan of God is right on time. It's coming to pass right now. In the time that we are living, we have seen Israel reborn, regathered to its land, and Jerusalem given back to the Jews. We have seen gardens bloom in the desert. We have seen cities rebuilt. And now we have an unmistakable sign — Israel is now a great, mighty political force.

Time magazine, July 4, 1988, in an article entitled "A Deadly New Missile Game," includes a map. This map shows Soviet and Chinese missiles coming out of Syria, Iraq, Saudi Arabia, and Egypt, all aimed at Israel. In the article it asks why all these countries would have these missiles aimed at Israel. Here's why: They see Israel as the most dominant force in the Middle East.

In Ezekiel 37:16-17, we find another great indicator: *"Moreover, thou son of man, take thee one stick, and write upon it, For Judah, and for the children of Israel his companions: then take another stick, and write upon it, For Joseph, the stick of Ephraim, and for all the house of Israel his companions: And join them one to another into one stick; and they shall become one in thine hand."* This says that when Israel is again a nation, when they are a great military power, they will be united from two nations to one stick, a united Israel. What a fulfillment God has allowed us to see. When Israel came back as a nation in 1948, they did not come back as Judah and Israel; they came back as a united Israel, exactly as the Bible predicted some twenty-five hundred years ago.

We are living in the last days. We know we are living in the last days because of the fulfillment of Bible prophecies. Other predictors and soothsayers can make their predictions, but they are only right five or ten percent of the time. The Bible is one hundred percent accurate. The Bible said that before Christ comes to set up His millennial kingdom, there will be a time of tribulation. And I believe the Bible teaches that before the tribulation will come, Israel will fulfill some very distinct prophecies. Among those is that when Israel came back, they would not be Judah and Israel, but they would be a united Israel.

Israel was divided after Saul, David, and Solomon. The descendants of Solomon saw the kingdom of Israel divided, split. That kingdom remained split until 1948. When they came back as a nation, they came back not as two nations, but as one, exactly as the Bible predicted in Ezekiel 37:16-17.

My dear friend, what more will God have to show us that we are living in these last days? I believe that we are living in the last days because of how God has so mightily fulfilled His Word concerning the nation of Israel.

Chapter Eight
The New Age Aspect

by Rob Lindsted

For a number of years, the New Age movement has just been a phrase that people have given to certain kinds of thinking. But today, I am impressed as I see how it has made great inroads into a number of areas, including scientific advancement. It has also made its way into our thinking in terms of advertisement, entertainment, and education. The business world is being affected by it. And the New Age movement is actually making inroads into the church. Maybe this is the most alarming of all. So how do we know we are living in the last days?

I would say it is because of the great deception that is going on among the very people that ought to be able to recognize the New Age movement as a sign that we are living in the last days.

In Matthew 24, Jesus says: *". . . Take heed that no man deceive you. For many shall come in my name, saying, I am Christ; and shall deceive many. . . . And many false prophets shall rise, and shall deceive many. . . . For there shall arise false Christs, and false prophets, and shall shew great signs and wonders; insomuch that, if it were possible, they shall deceive the very elect"* (Matt. 24:4-5, 11, 24). The description in the Bible of the last days deals with the idea of deception and with people that ought to know better who actually believe the lie of the devil. That lie has been packaged and sold to us in the form of the New Age movement.

I think we can see its impact even in terms of science. I am an engineer and a scientist. I don't believe that science itself is bad, but how it is sometimes can be. For example, I look at advances that are taking place right now that would allow for a one-world system. In Revelation 13, it mentions that when the Antichrist comes to power, it will be possible for him to mark people in such a way that every individual, small and great, rich and poor, buyer and seller, will be identified in some way. For years we wondered how this could be done. But recently, with the advent of the high-speed computer, we see that it is now possible. Not only is it possible, but because of other advances in science, it is probable.

I have an article about a small computer chip about the size of a grain of rice or a piece of sand. On this tiny computer chip, which would be embedded under the skin, there would be enough information to identify any individual who had one. It would be a wonderful way to code every person. Is it possible? Are people even considering it?

Again, I have an article written several years ago. The man who invented this little device is thrilled. He said: "I probably get three major phone calls a day from all over the world from people with new ideas for this technology." While it was a dream four or five years ago, today it is a reality.

This small electronic device can be implanted under the skin of an animal to observe its migration pattern. It can be embedded under the scales of a fish for the same purpose. They are placed on railroad cars in some areas for identification. In some cities, they actually implant these into pets, so they can be more easily traced when found missing.

Recently a doctor and an engineer working together, as reported in *American Medical News*, January 1988, produced a scenario in which a young child is kidnapped, identified with a small electronic device, and located within minutes. The Bureau for Missing Children says this is a great idea. We can now identify people wherever they are. While there are certain advantages to this, the technology that is needed to fulfill Revelation 13 is here today.

The article goes on to say that not only would it be good for missing children, but would also work for those that are aging. There may come a day in this country when you must be embedded with a little electronic device before you can collect Social Security.

The Boeing Company has now placed a little device such as this on the badge of every employee. Other companies are proposing embedding this little device somewhere on the body of their employees so that as they go into and out of confidential areas, their identity and the time they were in the area will be known. Don't you see that the technology is here today to do exactly what the Bible predicted nineteen hundred years ago?

In the February 20, 1989 issue of *Time* magazine, there is an ad in which two robots converse. This ad, sponsored by a major engineering firm, asks you to imagine a generation of robots that can learn from their experiences and make their own decisions. It shows a robotic father saying: "When I was your age, robots did what they were told." The son says: "But, Dad, my generation is different." Why does this come about? Because of the great advances we have seen in terms of computers.

It is now the talk of those involved with robotics to implant into these robots biological-type materials so robots can begin to make decisions independent of the investigator. Some people are calling this the second genesis. They say we have now created a man. As a result of creating another being, they believe we have become gods ourselves. This is the thinking of the New Age.

I also believe that we are in the last days because of the claims made by those involved in the New Age. A spokesman for the New Age said that while 1988 was the year of disaster (he points out predictions they made concerning air crashes and earthquakes which were fulfilled), the year 1989 was the year of disclosure. They said that among the things that would happen would be recognition of Japan for its great economy. They looked for the Japanese stock market to collapse. While those things were alarming, it was nothing like their prediction that 1989 could be the year for the declaration of the christ. Clearly, they are advocating that their time is now set.

In Revelation 17 and 18, the Bible says that in the last days there would be a revived Roman Empire. In Daniel 7 and 8 we find that this revived Roman Empire will take the form of thirteen nations. But when the Antichrist comes to power, three of those nations will be pulled out. I look at England and Margaret Thatcher and wonder if maybe it is one of the nations that will be pulled out. Then I read a headline that says: "An Even Dozen." This article talks about Spain and Portugal, when they joined the European Economic Community, brought the number of nations to twelve. Since the Bible says that when the Antichrist comes to power there will be thirteen with three removed, leaving ten, I really believe that we are on the verge of this.

In *Telemarketing* magazine, April 1989, the editor writes: "Europe 1992 — An Opportunity Or a Real Pitfall?" It asks how this will work. He says: *"A United Europe will need a leader, only one overall leader to function effectively."* Do you see the prediction? They are even predicting that if the Common Market had one overall effective leader, it could accomplish in 1992 what they have been hoping to do.

Recently, I read with amazement some of the predictions for 1992. *Northwest Airlines* magazine, talks about how the Common Market has grown to maturity and is actually ahead of pace, and how they expect it to be a great world power by that very year.

"A Unified Europe" is the title of an article out of

the *Wichita Beacon.* This article talks about a true Common Market by 1992. Not only is it possible, but it is probable and practical. Don't you see that we are living in exactly the conditions predicted by the Bible hundreds of years ago?

How do we know we are living in the last days? Because the political and scientific vehicles that the New Age movement needs to take over a one-world system is now in effect. Even before Christ calls the church home the scientific vehicle to mark, label, and identify every person is in effect today. The technology is here. And the political vehicle to control the world under a one-world system, I believe, is here. With their claims and predictions that this could well be the year, my dear friends, we ought to be looking for the coming of Christ.

In *Forbes* magazine, March 6, 1989, there is an article on the Common Market entitled "Friend Or Foe?" This article talks about how the Common Market is really a revived Roman Empire and how it really is committing itself to the new thinking and new philosophy of today. It says it is "a dream which may soon come true." It even reprints an article written thirty years ago giving the expectations of the Common Market. Now, thirty years later, they write that these expectations are being fulfilled. This says to me that the scientific and political vehicles for the one-world system are already intact.

I read advertisements all the time. Our own government, in an advertisement for the army, says: "Be all you can be." That's New Age thinking, isn't it? And yet, we've accepted that. And life insurance companies say: "You can move mountains. There's nothing you can't do, with the right resources and the right guidance." That is New Age thinking. The idea that we, by the power of our own mind, can control our destiny and create our future, is ridiculous.

Shirley MacLaine has become a hero. She has become a hero for advocating the New Age. Her articles concerning her rebirth and her reincarnation are becoming more accepted than even the Bible.

Seventeen magazine tells young girls how to mellow out, meditate, and say softly to themselves, "I am, I am." These are the exact words of God to Moses. Cartoons, television, and even our educational system try to tell our children that they are gods, that they are perfect beings. Dear friends, these things are a set-up for the New Age thinking.

What about fashion and music? In *MacLean's* Canada's weekly news magazine, April 17, 1989, there is an ad that says: "The New Age spirit is sweeping the land." It is no longer just another quirky item on a health-food store bulletin, but the inner landscaping arts of crystal meditating, channeling, regressing into past lives, and rebirthing. Then it says: "Can fashion be far behind? New Age comes of age in clothing and accessories." Then it has a New Age must-read list, which includes: *Going Within — A Guide To Inner Transformation* by Shirley MacLaine, *Crystal Enlightenment, Powers Of Myths, Creative Visualization,* and *The New Age Catalog.* These have become accepted reading today.

I say: Lord, how long before You call the church home? I believe we are living in the last generation because I see the great inroads of the New Age. It has made its way in terms of science, political power, advertising, fashion, and music, which is now the rage. They say that ads must be in this vein if they are to make progress. Businesses are spending literally billions of dollars training young executives in New Age thinking. This has made its way into some of our greatest business schools, including Harvard and Stanford.

In the *Wichita Beacon*, February 1989, it mentions a Wichita medical center that advocates vitamin therapy and power pyramids. People are brought into a pyramid-shaped building. Using powers inside that pyramid, they discuss cures for cancer. I look at this and say: Why are they so bold and why are we so timid?

But the inroads of the New Age into the church may be the most frightening. Recently, I began to see the claims of the New Age. They teach that you create your own destiny through the powers of the mind. Openly, the New Age admits that for most Americans, the New Age seems to be a harmless mix of Shirley MacLaine, channelers, and crystals. But they say that for a small number of Christians, they see this as a spiritual and psychological warfare. I am among those Christians. It is nothing less than the work of Satan, and I really believe that this is exactly true.

Among the things that the New Age advocates is that Jesus Christ was not and is not the only Christ, nor was He God. They say that God is an impersonal, cosmic god of energy forces. They say that man is himself god, for he consists of and created the forces. They say that man should seek and accept spiritual instruction directly from the spirit world. My dear friend, that should be a warning to us that we are living in the last days.

They say that all religions and religious teachings lead to the same goal. All have equal merit. They claim that the ancient wisdom of Babylon, including Egypt and Greece, not the Bible, is the basis of all truth. And they advocate that sin and evil do not exist.

Recently on talk shows I have heard New Age advocates claim that it is wrong for us to talk about sin. What is sin? Who sets the standards? And no longer do they see the Bible as setting the standards, but make their own standards because they are gods themselves. Unfortunately, this is sweeping its way into the church.

The New Age has indicated that they will gain an overall acceptance, they will make inroads, and unite all religions by dropping doctrine; by no longer insisting on the Word of God as the only standard, because other writings are equal; and, by no longer insisting upon the deity of God. When we talked about these things several years ago, especially dropping doctrine, everyone said that it would never happen. But recently, I saw in a church bulletin an alarming announcement. A major denomination in this country is now sponsoring a program on renewal in evangelism. They say:

"We welcome to our denomination a new story

*to tell. It will be a great evanglism of thrust and
it is called 'The New Age Dawning.' "*

I could hardly believe it. They have even named it
the same name. Why do we know that we are living in the
last days? Because the New Age has made great inroads
into all of society. It is now able to do what it promised
to do.

I know of places that now use Sunday school
material that no longer teaches against sin, but elevates
man. They are more concerned with our self-image than
that we are sinners. I really believe that one of the
detriments of the gospel today is that people are no
longer willing to say: "I am a sinner. I need God's
forgiveness." My dear friend, unless we are sinners, how
can we be forgiven by the blood of Jesus Christ? How
can we receive Christ as Savior?

I was appalled recently by a bulletin from a church
in Wichita, Kansas. They had a Mid-America Prayer
Summit. In the announcement concerning this, it says:

*"We have no one to represent but Jesus Christ;
nothing to promote but prayer; and, no project
to launch but to love Kansas."*

We ought to be loving God, shouldn't we? It says
they are going to do this ". . . in one of the mightiest
ways we can, that is, praying together." It says they are
going to emphasize church unity. They are going to
bring together a diverse team of charismatics, evangels,

Catholics, and protestants. The uniting faith is hearts that seek God, not doctrines or traditions. They are not satisfied on a local level; they want to go worldwide.

My dear friend, what we need to do is get back to the Word of God. We need to understand that Satan is paving a subtle inroad into the church. He is attacking us on every front.

I really believe that we are living in the last days. I believe that this could be the generation that will see Christ come back, because the New Age does not take its real effect until the tribulation begins. And before the tribulation ever begins, Christ will come for those that have received Him. Have you received Him? Has there ever been a time when by faith you admitted to God: "I am a sinner, and I accept what Jesus Christ did on the cross as payment for my sin"? My friend, there is no other way to salvation.

Chapter Nine

Russia and Israel
In the Last Days

by Emil Gaverluk

Last year, Defense and Energy Department officials acknowledged work had begun on a new family of "earth-penetrating" nuclear warheads for U.S. missiles. The purpose for the development of these high-tech warheads was to counteract the finding of the world's largest underground military base located near Sidon in Lebanon, on August 4, 1982. Russia has invested over four billion dollars worth of armaments into miles-long tunnels dug out forty-five feet wide by her giant earth-digging rotating machinery. This machinery is capable of even digging through hard rock.

Writing for the Associated Press, Norman Black states that former Defense Secretary Frank C. Carlucci said:

"The Soviet Union has been pursuing an 'enormously expensive' program of constructing huge underground bunkers and subways to

protect its leaders and allow them to fight a protracted nuclear war."

While the existence of such complexes has been known for years, only recently have we been able to do the full analysis of the enormous extent of this program of defense, hundreds of meters deep under several cities, interconnected with subway systems.

The defense secretary cited the underground work as just one example of how Soviet actions paint a different picture than the public statements of Kremlin leader Mikhail S. Gorbachev, with his emphasis on arms control initiatives and improving the economy.

Carlucci declared:

"There can be only one purpose for these shelters — to provide the Soviet leadership the ability to fight a protracted nuclear conflict. These facilities contradict in steel and concrete Soviet protestations that they share President Reagan's view that nuclear war can never be won and must never be fought."

Russia must have completed these tunnels in Lebanon by August 4, 1982. This would be especially true of those underground storage facilities and bunkers under Moscow and other important Russian cities since the tunnels were completed and stocked by that date.

It astonished the world when Israel launched an all-out attack upon the PLO in Lebanon in June of 1982, and in the process discovered these tunnels loaded to equip a point-army of one hundred thousand enemy soldiers for the purpose of attacking Israel. It seems evident that Russia was planning to launch this attack, even if it meant an all-out nuclear engagement, not only with Israel, but also with the West. It is ironic that God used this means to supply Israel with this outstanding military armament, without their having to pay one cent for it. I believe the leader of this Israeli invasion of Lebanon was Michael, the great archangel, ". . . *the great prince which standeth for the children of thy people . . .*" according to Daniel 12:1.

The world press did not trumpet the startling discovery and its portent. This discovery should have alerted all the nations of the world to its ominous significance. This was a signal for a third world war, with the advent of a nuclear holocaust. Yet, only one photographer showed up at this bizarre and frightening display of power, and he expressed astonishment that "not a single other world reporter showed up to see the largest cave being displayed to the public, which was several miles in total area, filled with armaments."

The world appeared to be blind to this awful threat that threatened her very existence. Even the American press seemed to be totally blind to this danger. The fact is, Israel saved the world from a third world war in 1982, and we have an extended grace period from God. It appears it will be coming to an end very soon, possibly even this year.

I say this because of the sudden emergence of a new

leader in Russia, who is furiously rushing around disarming the West of any fears of attack, or the use of nuclear arms. Also, the Soviets will soon deploy operational units of their new Blackjack long-range bomber, deployment of the new rail-mounted SS-24 nuclear missile has begun, and production should start soon for a more accurate version of the huge SS-18. Carlucci said the deployment of the SS-24 was significant, because it means the Soviets now have two operational ICBMs that are mobile, "while we're still arguing in Congress about whether or not we should have even one. . . ."

Gorbachev knows that Russia could launch only one huge hydrogen bomb by missile, explode it two hundred miles above the center of the United States, Omaha, Nebraska for example, and thus radiate gamma rays covering every square mile of the United States, Canada, and Mexico with fifty thousand volts of electrical energy. Similarly, if the United States explodes their one over Russia, it would cover all of European Russia, and territory into Siberia. The nation committing this act first, would have made a pre-emptive strike, gaining instantaneous advantage over the other. Everything electrical would be totally knocked out.

There is one thing that many on either side realizes, and that is God is still in control, and will not allow the breakout of the third world war until after the resurrection-rapture of all the world saints: the dead and the living. We are now living in the pre-tribulation days. The tribulation will start after the Antichrist makes his appearance and signs a peace treaty with many in Israel for seven years. Antichrist cannot appear until the northern confederacy, led by Russia, is destroyed on the mountains of Israel, according to Ezekiel 38 and 39. Russia cannot attack Israel until after the worldwide resurrection-rapture of the saints.

The rapture may occur on one of two Jewish festivals: Shavout or Rosh Hashanah. The departure of the body of Christ will leave a vast emptiness in the population of the world. The startling revelation of the bride of Christ is revealed in the Sermon on the Mount in Matthew 5:14 where Jesus states: *"Ye are the light of the world. . . ."* This is the first such revelation in the book of Matthew, a treatise designed especially with Israel in mind.

We picked up a wonderful little booklet, written by Dr. John Fischer, a Hebrew professor and author, at the Florida Bible Prophecy Conference. This booklet is entitled *The Meaning and Importance Of the Jewish Holidays.*

Let me quote a segment from the section on the holiday of Shavout:

> *"Messianic significance abounds in this festival. From God's perspective, the time of great 'harvest' — when large numbers of Jews and then Gentiles came into a personal relationship with Him — was initiated at the Shavout after Yeshua's (Jesus') resurrection (Acts 2:40-43). The two leavened (impure) loaves of*

*Shavout may therefore symbolize Jew and Gentile 'presented' to God and now are part of His 'family.' You may want to read Matthew 27:51-53 in this connection. I believe that Jesus escorted this group of resurrected Jewish saints and presented them to the Father as the firstfruits after they had witnessed to many in Jerusalem that Jesus truly was the Messiah-Savior. This was probably the reason for the astonishing response in Acts 2:41 which states: 'Then they that gladly received his word were baptized: and the same day were added **unto them about three thousand souls.'***

*"We also read in Acts 4:4: 'Howbeit many of them which heard the word believed: and the number of the men was about **five thousand**.' This was not counting the women and children."*

Now, let us look at Rosh Hashanah.

"It has deep messianic significance. The rabbis taught that one day the shofar would sound and the Messiah would come. When He came, the dead would rise (Joseph Hertz, Daily Prayer Book, p. 865) about a decade after Yeshua. Rav Shaul talked about this when he referred to the fact that Yeshua would return for His followers and would thereafter rule the Earth as Messiah the King. People refer to this even as the rapture or Yeshua's

second coming. In describing the rapture, the Apostle Paul said: 'The trumpet (shofar) will sound; the messiah will come, and the dead will rise' (1 Thess. 4:16-18). This day will certainly be characterized by joy, delight, and sweetness (count apples dipped in honey for their sweetness)."

J.R. Church who hosts the *Prophecy In the News* telecast weekly, wrote a fascinating chronological study of *Hidden Prophecies in the Psalms*. Notice how the year coincides with the number of each psalm.

Psalm 1: Appears to set the mind-set of world Jewry in 1901.

Psalm 2: The world is rushing headlong toward another series of wars. Prophecy by Jesus is found in Matthew 24:6.

Psalm 3: The sufferings of Israel in Russia.

Psalm 14: World War One.

Psalm 17: In 1917, British General Edmund Allenby captured Jerusalem without firing a shot, and he was a Christian. British Parliament passed the Balfour Declaration.

Psalm 18: Palestine should be opened to Jewish immigration.

Psalm 48: Rebirth of the nation of Israel.

Psalm 88: *"Wilt thou show wonders to the dead? Shall the dead arise and praise thee?"* (vs. 10).

Psalm 89: *"What man is he that liveth, and shall not see*

> *Death? Shall he deliver his soul from the hand of the grave?"* (vs. 48).

Psalm 90: *". . . and we fly away"* (vs. 10).

In other words, we are caught up to be with Christ in the air, and he takes us on a long journey up to where Satan is not allowed, because, if you read Isaiah 14:13, God says he wanted to put his throne above the start of God, and he was going to sit on the Mount of the Congregation. God did not allow Satan to do that. It was a holy place provided for the bride, the church and that's where we are going! Nobody knows the hour, the day, nor the year indicated in Psalms 88, 89, and 90. But we do have these clues given here. Will this be the year?

Let Us Live in the Probability of One of These Years

This means self-examination of our spiritual lives, for we are to meet Jesus in the air face to face, according to 1 Thessalonians 4:17, which reads: *"Then we which are alive and remain shall be caught up together with them in the clouds, to meet the* **Lord in the air: and so shall we ever be with the Lord."** We are changed from mortality to immortality. ***"Beloved, now are we the sons of God, and it doth not yet appear what we shall be: but we know that, when he shall appear, we shall be like him; for we shall see him as he is"*** (1 John 3:2).

How is He? He is absolutely perfect. And we are

going to be like Him, we also will be perfect. The resurrection-rapture comes first, then the Russians will invade Israel as they suddenly realize that the United States of America has lost approximately fifty to seventy million people, or possibly more. I believe that all children to the age of accountability will be caught up throughout the world, including the United States of America, which would increase the number considerably. Hurriedly, the Russians would determine how many they have lost in the rapture, and would come up with a rough estimate of four million adults plus another ten to fifteen million children. (These numbers are my guesses. The figures could be much larger.) They would say somthing like: "We haven't lost very many, but look at America! They are in a double dilemma. The rapture has made them very weak." The Russian military would seize the opportunity of the American confusion to launch the hydrogen nuclear bomb in space. It would explode far above Omaha, Nebraska, releasing the electromagnetic pulses of gamma rays which would strip North America of all its electrical power, adding to the confusion left by the rapture.

Our clues left to this scenario come from the exponential analysis of cascading events as preparations are made for the final showdown between Satan and the Lord Jesus. The Book of Revelation gives us a clear picture of the outcome, and its finality. *"And the devil that deceived them was cast into the lake of fire and brimstone, where the beast and the false prophet are, and shall be tormented day and night for ever and ever"*

(Rev. 20:10). **The final phase is about to begin.**

Since 1948, Israel has won every war. She must not lose one war or it is all over for her. It is through prophetic revelation Israel finds many of the truths necessary to cope with these modern times. With her, guiding her to every win, I believe is an invisible being whose name is Michael, the guardian angel.

Add to this that Israel has produced more scientists, musicians, and professors than any other nation on earth. They were made a gifted people, because ahead of them, in the near future, they will become the greatest nation on earth, ministering to the people of the world. No other nation can claim this kind of distinction — not even the United States of America.

The only book that tells of these future events and much more, is the Bible. It tells us that Israel will suffer much at the hands of the Gentiles, and many more prophecies will be fulfilled in the very near future regarding Israel. Yet, we owe a great debt to the Jewish people. Jewish descendants discovered antibiotics and other medications, surgical procedures, and great inventions. They are great mathematicians, musicians, philosophers, scientists, and so forth. They are not atheists or evolutionists, per se, since their background goes back to Abraham who believed God and was God's friend. *"Art not thou our God, who didst drive out the inhabitants of this land before thy people Israel, and gavest it to the seed of Abraham thy friend for ever?"* (2 Chron. 20:7). Israel is the only nation in the world to have received a direct prophetic revelation for her future existence.

In doing some research into the original words in several passages of scripture, I found this item of interest. Looking at the Hebrew and Chaldee dictionary in *Strong's Concordance of the Bible*, number 3260 is the Hebrew word *Y'diy*. In the English translations, this can be rendered "Jedi." The following definition is given: "Appointed; Jedi, an Israelite: — Iddo." The word "Jedi" means an Israelite.

In truth, the statement: "The Return of the Jedi" is real, and has been happening since 1948. It is God who will bring them back. In Isaiah 54:4, it says: *"Fear not; for thou shalt not be ashamed* [Heb. *buwsh:* to be ashamed; to be disappointed or delayed; confounded or confused; become dry]: *neither be thou confounded; for thou shalt not be put to shame: for thou shalt forget the shame of thy youth, and shalt not remember the reproach of thy widowhood any more."* I believe Israel is the wife of God, as indicated from many Old Testament scriptures.

"For thy Maker is thine husband; the Lord of hosts is his name; and thy Redeemer the Holy One of Israel; The God of the whole earth shall he be called. For the Lord hath called thee as a woman forsaken and grieved in spirit, and a wife of youth, when thou wast refused, saith thy God. For a small moment have I forsaken thee; but with great mercies will I gather thee" (Isa. 54:5-7).

Now read Isaiah 43:6-7: *"I will say to the north, Give up; and to the south, Keep not back: bring my sons from far, and my daughters from the ends of the earth; Even every one that is called by my name: for I have created him for my glory, I have formed him; yea, I have made him."*

Therefore, before Russia invades Israel, all the "Jedi" must return to their homeland. I believe this is being fulfilled in ways we cannot readily see, but have received many indications of through current events.

We have recently seen the Jews begin changing their attitudes toward Jesus Christ, the Messiah. There is a remarkable book written by a prominent Jewish Christian physician, Arthur W. Kac, M.D. I quote from the back cover.

> *"The book,* The Messiahship Of Jesus *examines the attitudes of modern-day Jews toward Jesus. . . . This book will challenge you with statements about Jesus by prominent Jews (rabbis, theologians, scientists, professors, writers, journalists), analyses by Hebrew Christians of present-day Jewish attitudes toward Jesus based on the teachings of the Old and New Testaments. . . . Many will find the most important essays to be those by six Jewish Christians who will tell why and how they became followers of Jesus."*

I wept as I read this book. The emotions and feelings behind the classical English wording, so descriptive and filled with yearning for the Messiah, overflowed into my being. You will feel it with a deep longing and penitent prayer that will bring you close to the Messiah and prepare you for his soon-coming. You should look for this book, get it soon, read it carefully, and then determine to talk to your Jewish friends about it. The fact that this book was recently written indicates how near we are to the second coming of the Lord.

My own recent book, *The Rapture Before the Russian Invasion of Israel*, is being offered on radio, television, and even satellite worldwide. We know the Lord is using this means, among many others, to alert Christians to the nearness of His coming. There is a surge of excitement and interest in research relative to the resurrection-rapture by believers.

In recent developments at the Hebrew University in Jerusalem, some twenty Israeli rabbinical scholars are decoding the Torah numerically by computer. Journalist Phil Brennan wrote an unusual article in the prestigious *London Sunday Mail*. Hidden codes have been uncovered by this team they say prove the existence of God — and they want to keep their mind-boggling discovery a secret, because they fear the effect it might have on mankind! According to the *Mail's* Jonathan Margolis, Israeli Rabbi David Ordman confined details of his amazing discovery to a meeting held in London.

Rabbi David Ordman, who directed the five-year computer study of the first five books of the Bible — known in Judaism as the Torah — said that his team had found a series of hidden codes buried deep within the original text, written twenty-four hundred years ago.

The codes are so complex, it took thousands of

computer hours to unmask them. It would have required an ultra-modern, high-tech computer to devise them and hide them in the text — an obvious impossibility twenty-four hundred years ago.

The Torah, therefore, could only have been written by someone given explicit, divine direction on how it was to be done, Rabbi Ordman stressed. He suggested that the texts were encoded as a **sign to future generations that the Torah is much more than a history of the roots of the ancient Jewish people, but instead is a time capsule awaiting a generation with the advanced technology to decode its content.**

Scholars, he said, have long noticed that the number seven has a mystical significance. For example, all the key names in Genesis — such as God, Adam, and Noah — are always mentioned seven times!

Other examples of this: Starting with the first letter "T" in Genesis, and counting every forty-ninth letter (seven times seven), the word Torah is spelled out.

In Exodus, if you start with the first "Y" and then add every seventh letter, the Hebrew name of God — "Yehovah" — is spelled out. Using these and other examples of the number seven's key importance, Rabbi Ordman and his colleagues programmed all one hundred twenty-five thousand words in the Torah and combed through billions of combinations — a job that would have taken humans hundreds of years to complete without computers.

To their amazement, they found that the Bible contains numerous messages hidden in number codes, the significance of which they have yet to fully understand. In a forty-three word passage in Genesis, the names of thirty-one trees are encoded in the text, actually identifying the types of trees that grew in the garden of Eden!

"To plan this kind of thing would take years," according to Rabbi Ordman. *"And they had to prepare a text as well, with perfect grammar, a message, and with no contradictions."*

"We are not trying to prove the divinity of the Torah here, but the statistical odds against it being humanly written are impossible!" Publicity at this early stage of his work, he warned, might change the world before the world is ready for it.

What thrills me is that this discovery was made by this team of biblical researchers and their computer, totally unaware of a similar discovery by Dr. Ivan Panin, mathematician and professor at Harvard in the 1890s into the first quarter of the twentieth century. He got so excited about this subliminal language in the Bible that he spent fifteen hours every day researching not with a computer, since there were none, but with pencil and paper. Needless to say, when he started this project, the enormity of identity and recognition by numbers so startled him, he fell on his knees and pled with the Lord for forgiveness and acceptance of the Lord Jesus as his personal Savior. As his faith grew, the deeper he involved himself in the midst of the conference speeches he made, and he continued pursuing the revelation in an inexhaustible base of information, the

Bible.

Wait until Dr. Ordman's team discovers that the name of Jesus in the Greek New Testaments adds out to 888. Then to their astonishment, they will discover that the Hebrew does the same thing for the Second Person of the Trinity. I predict this will be the point of their conversion and acceptance of Jesus as their Messiah. The computers will reveal this startling development by their own hands.

Here are some of the New Testament subliminal numerics. In the Greek, Jesus' name is spelled as followes: "Iota (10), Eta (8), Sigma (200), Omicron (70), Upsellon (400), Sigma (200) — IESOUS."The sum of the preceding numbers adds up to 888.

In the Hebrew of the Old Testament, a subliminal numeric language appears in Isaiah 52:10 which reads: *"The Lord hath made bare his holy arm in the eyes of all the nations; and all the ends of the earth shall see the salvation of our God."* "Salvation of" equals 786; "our God" equals 102; both add up to two Hebrew words revealing the number 888.

First, let me tell you the importance of 888 in the Old Testament. To the Jew, Saturday is the Sabbath. Jesus arose from the grave, not on the seventh day, but on the eighth day. Each Sunday, we celebrate his resurrection. Add to this that his number is not just 8, but 888. This is in contrast to the number of Antichrist, which is 666. Three eights signifies **the Holy Trinity**. This reveals Jesus' divinity. He is God in the flesh. It was no coincidence that the book that will sustain Israel through the tribulation period, announces clearly in Isaiah 9:6-7: *"For unto us a child is born, unto us a son is given: and the government shall be upon his shoulder: and his name shall be called Wonderful, Counseller, The mighty God, the everlasting Father, The Prince of Peace. Of the increase of his government and peace there shall be no end, upon the throne of David, and upon his kingdom, to order it, and to establish it with judgment and with justice from henceforth even for ever. The zeal of the Lord of hosts will perform this."*

To support this, we now search out the Old Testament references that subliminally reveal the number for Jesus, 888. Ezra 2:62-63 has an astonishing revelation as to who is the real High Priest. No such high priest ever again appeared in Israel. Jesus is the High Priest, the real Messiah. The Hebrew word for "a priest" has the numeric value of 75; "with Urim," 287; "and Thummim," 526; the total is 888.

The book of John refers to Jesus as the Word made flesh. He also is referred to as the King and Savior of Israel. Deuteronomy begins with "these be the words" made of two Hebrew words equaling 207; the last two words close with "all Israel" equaling 591; together they add to 888.

The equation I like best is found in Malachi 3:6: *"For I am the Lord* [Jehovah], *I change not. . . ."* Four Hebrew words spell out "I am" which equals 61; "Jehovah" equals 26; "not" equals 31; "I change not" equals 770. The total produces the number 888.

So obviously, God has a time when the Old

Testament is going to be revealed speaking to them about 888. And they will have to recognize that who they are talking about is none other than the one who came two thousand years ago. That was the Lord Jesus Christ. Now, a day is as a thousand years, and a thousand years is as a day. We are about to conclude the two thousand years from the look of things. If that is the case, then again, here is another way we can look at the fact that we must be very close to the time of the Lord's coming. I believe He is coming very soon. So it behooves us to walk closely with the Lord, to open the Bible, and to read it. It was a thrill to me as I discovered these truths. I have grown in grace and strength and faith in the Lord Jesus. This is so important.

The shout of the saints, the trumpet sound will soon occur, and we must be ready. I am not setting dates, I am not a date setter, but I do know the signs of the times point to His soon return.

Chapter Ten

The Sexual Revolution —
Party's Over

by N.W. Hutchings

Dr. Ward Gates of the U.S. Centers for Disease Control is quoted in the August 12, 1985 edition of *Newsweek* as saying of the deadly disease AIDS:

"Looking ahead, anyone can see the potential for this disease being much worse than anything mankind has seen before."

This is a rather amazing statement, especially in view of the past plagues and diseases that have infected mankind. Let us consider, for example, the Spanish flu epidemic of 1918-19 in which over five hundred thousand Americans were killed and twenty million died worldwide from this one plague alone. In 1848 a million Russians died of cholera. The Black Death, or Bubonic Plague, killed one-third of the human population living between India and Iceland in just two years — 1348-50. We could continue to quote statistics from the annals of medical history relating to the hundreds of millions who died from smallpox, malaria, yellow fever, and other microscopic killers of mankind, but such numbers begin to lose their meaning. We could go back even further in biblical history and refer to such cases as the judgments of God upon Egypt that terminated with the killing of the firstborn of each family. But none of these past plagues, judgments, or diseases strikes as much terror in the hearts and minds of the experts, those afflicted, and the general population, as today's judgment, AIDS, because AIDS is the only total killer in the history of mankind, as far as microscopic diseases are concerned. No one to this date has ever recovered from AIDS. It is one hundred percent fatal. It is an attack upon the present social order of mankind.

Today, man seems to be looking every place — the test tubes, the microscopes, the medical laboratories, even in the social and moral patterns of contemporary humanity. The answer is not there. We propose the answer is to be found in God's Holy Word, the Bible. Jesus prophesied of the days of His coming again: *"For nation shall rise against nation, and kingdom against kingdom: and there shall be famines, and pestilences, and earthquakes, in divers places. All these are the beginning of sorrows"* (Matt. 24:7-8). Our Lord prophesied that in the last days wars would increase, both in scope and intensity; this has happened in the twentieth century. He also said there would be famines; famines are increasing in Africa, Asia, South America, and the world is set for the greatest famine it has ever experienced as the population runs out of control. Jesus said there would be earthquakes in divers places, and earthquakes are increasing. Just a few years ago, an earthquake just to the east and south of Peking in China killed almost one million people. In September 1985, the great earthquake in Mexico City occurred. Recently there have been tragic earthquakes in Russia and all over the face of the globe. As Dr. Carl Baugh brought out in a former message in this series, the world is right for the greatest earthquake it has ever experienced.

But Jesus also said there would be judgments of pestilences and great disease epidemics, indicating these would be worse than man has ever witnessed before. In conclusion, He said: *"Men's hearts failing them for fear, and for looking after those things which are coming on the earth . . ."* (Luke 21:26).

To understand the fatalistic dilemma that infests the present generation, we return to the beginning, to the garden of Eden. When God divided Adam into two separate and distinct personalities, man and woman, He ordained that a man should cleave unto his wife, a wife cleave unto her her husband, and they should be one flesh (Gen. 2:24). Any deviation from God's ordination of this sexual relationship between a man and a woman was forbidden; it would be considered sin and result in judgment. However, we read in Genesis 6 that the "sons of God," whom we interpret to be fallen angels, took wives from the daughters of men. The result of this genetic contamination is described in Genesis 6:4-7: *"There were giants in the earth in those days; and also after that, when the sons of God came in unto the daughters of men, and they bare children to them. . . . And God saw that the wickedness of man was great in the earth, and that every imagination of the thoughts of his heart was only evil continually. And it repented the Lord that he had made man on the earth, and it grieved him at his heart. And the Lord said, I will destroy man whom I have created from the face of the earth. . . ."*

That the judgment of God brought upon the Antediluvians was the result of a massive sexual contamination is verified in 2 Peter 2:4-6: *"For if God spared not the angels that sinned, but cast them down to hell. . . . And spared not the old world, but saved Noah the eighth person, a preacher of righteousness, bringing in the flood upon the world of the ungodly; And turning the cities of Sodom and Gomorrah into ashes condemned them with an overthrow, making them an ensample unto those that after should live ungodly."* Evidence of the reason of the judgment of the flood, and again at Sodom and Gomorrah, is also provided in Romans 1 and Jude 1:6-8: *"And the angels which kept not their first estate, but left their own habitation, he hath reserved in everlasting chains under darkness unto the judgment of the great day. Even as Sodom and Gomorrah, and the cities about them in like manner, giving themselves over to fornication, and going after strange flesh, are set forth for an example, suffering the vengeance of eternal fire."*

The reason God considers homosexuality an abomination is because it is an attack upon the created order of all things. Fornication is an attack upon the basic union of civilization, the family. So God looks upon adultery and homosexuality as two of the greatest abominations.

Once more the biblical evidence is presented that sexual promiscuity, sexual fornication, unrestrained sexual intercourse outside of marriage, and especially sexual deviations always bring about national and/or universal judgment. God points out to us in His Word that there are sufficient examples of this in the past, so as to leave all mankind without excuse.

But Jesus said again in Matthew 24:37: *"But as the days of Noe were, so shall also the coming of the Son of man be."* It is our understanding of both the Hebrew and King James Version text that where we read in Genesis 6:9 that *". . . Noah was a just man and perfect in his generations . . ."* it means that the immediate family of Noah was the only group of persons that had escaped the genetic contamination brought on by a worldwide defiance of the will of God concerning the created order. Our God is not a God who would have destroyed innocent people in the flood, and concerning past judgments, Peter wrote in his second epistle: *"The Lord is not slack concerning his promise, as some men count slackness; but is longsuffering to us-ward, not willing that any should perish, but that all should come to repentance. But the day of the Lord will come as a thief in the night . . ."* (2 Pet. 3:9-10).

At the beginning of our twentieth century, 1900 A.D., in the United States — according to the *1985 World Almanac* — about one in every fifteen marriages ended in divorce. But the divorce rate began to increase until 1987, the latest year for which we have statistics, when there were 2,421,000 marriages and 1,157,000 divorces, clearly indicating that now one in every two marriages ends in divorce. Even so, this is not the entire story because so many couples live together without getting married and then separate without a record of divorce. So the sexual conditions in our day parallel those in the days of Noah.

In the 1950s and 1960s, the Western world entered the age of the sexual revolution. The sexual revolution was and is the result of the following social, economic, political, and moral changes:

1. The industrial revolution which resulted in changing the woman's role in the home and society.
2. The increase of wars in intensity and scope.
3. New developments in communications, especially movies and television programs that glorify sex.
4. The teaching of "situation ethics" in public schools and higher institutions of learning.
5. Birth control drugs and devices that allow a woman to engage in promiscuity without getting pregnant.
6. Abortion, which further freed a woman from giving birth — even if she became pregnant.
7. The general failure of the clergy to denounce fornication, adultery, and homosexuality as sin.
8. Rampant homosexuality.

The result has been five major diseases that threaten

the very existence of our social order. The violation of God's commandments concerning the relationship between the sexes, with the sure judgment that follows for disobedience, was evident in the days of Noah — and again at Sodom and Gomorrah. Archaeologists have reported that the Canaanite tribes whom God commanded that Israel destroy were heavily infected with venereal diseases. Even their children were infected. It is thought by some historians that Alexander the Great, a bisexual, died from such a cause. Then we could walk on down through history to cite Henry the Eighth, Napoleon, and many other prominent personalities who were thought to have suffered or died from such causes. Repeatedly, we see God's judgment against even the world's most prominent personalities for this sin. No nation, no person, regardless of education, political standing, or economic status, is exempt. The five major judgments against God's established order between the sexes is evident through the diseases that infect mankind today:

1. Gonorrhea
2. Syphillis
3. Herpes
4. Chlamydia
5. AIDS

During the moral decline of the Roman Empire, herpes was so prevalent that one emperor, Tiberius, banned kissing in public because so many of the Romans had lip sores from this disease. Most of these diseases go all the way back, all except one — AIDS. AIDS is the one new disease that has appeared in these last days. And it is the most terrible. The sexual revolution was really a moral revolution which we believe has produced this disease. It was a spiritual revolt against God and Judeo-Christian standards of morality. Nowhere has this war been waged more blatantly and fiercely than in the homosexual world. Gays, both homosexual males and lesbians, began to come out of the closet. They waged demonstrations, and lobbied on city, state, and national levels to remove all laws that would prevent the acceptance of homosexuality as simply an "alternative lifestyle." But God condemns this abomination in both sexes; He judges it to be the most abominable of all sins that men or women commit. We read in Leviticus 18:22-30 that any man or woman who would indulge in such abominations should be killed or deserved death, and any nation that allowed such a practice would be destroyed from the face of the earth.

We read in Romans 1:26-27, 32: *"For this cause God gave them up unto vile affections: for even their women did change the natural use into that which is against nature: And likewise also the men, leaving the natural use of the woman, burned in their lust one toward another; men with men working that which is unseemly, and receiving in themselves that recompence of their error. . . . Who knowing the judgment of God, that they which commit such things are worthy of death, not only do the same, but have pleasure in them that do them."*

When the "gay" movement came to the full in the 1970s, it would seem that God intervened. Homosexual men began dying from AIDS. AIDS is a disease spread by homosexual acts of men. Of the 11,132 cases of AIDS reported in *Time* magazine, August 12, 1985, seventy-eight percent were male homosexuals; fifteen percent were drug addicts who had contracted the disease through hypodermic needles; one percent were hemophiliacs who possibly got AIDS through blood transfusions; five percent were classified as "others" or unknown; one percent were heterosexual men and women; and, one percent contracted AIDS through blood transfusions. So, we see that the major cause of AIDS is still homosexuality and the transmission of AIDS by drug addicts through the sharing of needles.

It would seem again that as it was before the flood at Sodom and Gomorrah, at Rome, and all previous empires that have fallen from moral decay, God is warning America to repent or perish. The answer to all of these plagues which threaten the very existence of our nation is given in 2 Chronicles 7:14: *"If my people, which are called by my name, shall humble themselves, and pray, and seek my face, and turn from their wicked ways; then will I hear from heaven, and will forgive their sin, and will heal their land."*

We believe the evidence of these diseases, these terrible plagues, give testimony that we are living in the last days and that Jesus could come at any time.

Frequently, we are asked if we are really living in

the last days what we, as Christians, should be doing. The expected answer is that we can come up with some miraculous plan of action that will change people and circumstances so that everything will be all right. However, there is no miracle solution to the social, moral, and political problems of today. There never has been in the past.

Let us consider Noah. Noah knew the judgment of the flood was coming. Unless God showed mercy, that entire generation would be destroyed. But there was absolutely nothing that Noah could do except that which God told him to do. He built an ark; he preached righteousness. But he had no converts outside his own household.

Next, let us consider Lot. Lot was informed that God was going to destroy Sodom and Gomorrah. What did poor Lot do? He did the best he could by pleading with the men to forsake their sexual abominations. He even offered them his daughters. But only he and a couple of family members were saved.

Let us also consider Jeremiah. The prophet Jeremiah witnessed to the nation of Israel in a time of idolatry and immorality. Judgment was eminent. He went through the streets of Jerusalem preaching repentance and righteousness. But about the only evident result was to get himself thrown in a dungeon.

Jesus Christ pronounced judgment upon the generation of Israel of His day when He ministered in Israel. Peter and John were called to witness to this generation after His death, resurrection, and ascension. What did

Peter and John do? They did what they were instructed to do. They preached the message: *"Repent, and be baptized every one of you . . . for the remission of sins . . ."* (Acts 2:38). Some believed, but most did not. And judgment fell upon that generation.

We believe we are in the last days, and if so, the judgments of the tribulation loom menacingly in the future. In these last days, we believe the Scriptures call us to, like Noah, condemn the world of sin through our own testimony, our own righteous witness. We are called to be ambassadors for Christ, to tell others of the saving Gospel so that some may flee from the wrath to come and be saved. And, above all, as Paul declared, to be patient, to be witnessing, to be working, to warn others, to be ready for the coming of the Lord, and then to wait for God's Son from heaven.

Chapter Eleven

If These Really Are the Last Days, What Shoud We Do

by William Sillings

Rather than draw further attention to why I believe these are the last days, this chapter asks: "In light of my faith that these *are* the last days, what should I do?"

There is an old story about a man who went to visit the proprietor of a large estate. Finding the proprietor absent, he asked the gardener: "When will your master return home?" The gardener answered kindly: "I'm sorry, I don't know, sir. He's away on a business trip and did not say when He would return." Looking around, the visitor said: "You certainly are doing a good job with the gardening. This place is beautiful. In fact," said the visitor, "you're caring for the lawn and gardens as though you expect your master might return tomorrow." "Well, thank you, sir," replied the gardener, "but actually, I'm caring for them as though He might return today."

That is an accurate picture of the attitude the Christian should have in light of the faith that these are the last days. For while we do not know when the Lord will return, we know that He shall, and we need to be ready when He comes again. In speaking of the consummation of all things, 2 Peter 3:11 states: *"Seeing then that all these things shall be dissolved, what manner of persons ought ye to be in all holy conversation and godliness?"* That is the question we face today. What is our responsibility since we do believe these really are the last days?

Let's approach that question from two distinct perspectives and ask two personal questions. First, let's deal with the question: "What should I do in order to prepare myself in the last days?" Then, let's look at: "What should I be doing to help prepare the world for the last days?" In order to answer those questions, I wish to draw your attention to a few of the many scriptures regarding this subject. Let's look first at the question of what I should be doing to prepare myself.

First, I need to be sure that I am one of God's children, that I have on the wedding garment. In Matthew 23:11-12, Jesus gave the parable of the great wedding feast a king made for his son. Everyone at the feast was required to wear the wedding garment. As a result of Christ's vicarious sacrifice on Calvary, the wedding garment for the marriage supper of the Lamb is provided for us. We must have it on to be admitted.

Therefore, if you have never become a Christian by trusting in Christ as your personal Savior, I urge you to do so today. Do not put off such a decision. For, as the Hebrew writer said: *"Today is the day of salvation, now* is the accepted time." How is this done? By repenting of all your sins and believing on the Lord Jesus Christ. Romans 10:9-10 says: *". . . if thou shalt confess with thy mouth the Lord Jesus, and shalt believe in thine heart that God hath raised him from the dead, thou shalt be saved. For with the heart man believeth unto righteousness; and with the mouth confession is made unto salvation."* John 1:12 says: *". . . as many as received him, to them gave he power to become the sons of God, even to them that believe on his name."* So, my friend, if you have not done so yet, please bow your head in prayer, confess your sins and your need of Christ, believe on Him, and make Him the Lord of your life. Then you will have put on the wedding garment, and will be prepared for the coming of the Lord. Oh, what a blessed privilege — to be born of God and made ready!

But even if we call ourselves Christians, we need to be sure that it is the wedding garment of Christ that clothes us, and not our natural goodness or our own righteousness. It must be the garment Christ has provided if we are to be prepared.

Not only do I need to be sure I have donned the wedding garment; but, like the gardener awaiting his master's return, I need to live in a state of continual readiness for Christ's return. In the parable of the wise and foolish virgins in Matthew 25, Jesus taught that those who are counted worthy to enter the marriage feast will be wise enough to be fully prepared. The five wise virgins were able to enter for the wedding because they were careful to take enough oil with them. But five were foolish. They did not take care to observe the status of their preparation. Consequently, they were not able to enter into the wedding. Like the five wise virgins, we need to keep ourselves prepared for the bridegroom's coming. Let us observe at least the following five steps which will help us do that.

1. *Guard against sinful living.* We are to be set apart unto God. Our text in 2 Peter suggests that in view of the coming of the day of God we are to live holy and godly in our conduct. In His great high priestly prayer, Jesus prayed that His disciples should be sanctified through the truth. He also prayed that they might be kept from the evil that is in the world. And thank God, His prayer was not only for those disciples in that day, but was also for everyone who should believe on Him through their words. That means His prayer was for us today.

   Furthermore, the Apostle Paul warned us to pay close attention to our spiritual lives when he wrote, *". . . your adversary the devil, as a roaring lion, walketh about, seeking whom he may devour"* (1 Pet. 5:8). Because of this, he commands, *" . . .be sober, be vigilant."* That is, be serious-minded and alert. The imperative in the original text rings sharply: "Stay awake! Be alert!." Our faith and confidence in God must not result in spiritual slackness. We need to guard ourselves diligently while trusting our eternal salvation to the Master and Savior of our souls.

2. *Watch for Christ's return.* Our text says that the day

of the Lord will come as a thief in the night. The words of Jesus in Matthew 24:42 and 44 further establish this truth: *"Watch therefore: for ye know not what hour your Lord doth come. . . . Therefore be ye also ready: for in such an hour as ye think not the Son of man cometh."* To watch in this passage means to give diligent attention to the things that point to His coming and to be ready. Again, we do not know when He is returning, but He will return. Hebrews 9:28 says that when He comes, He shall appear *". . . unto them that look for him. . . ."* So, let us watch continually for His return.

3. *Avoid the tendency to grow weary of waiting.* In the parable of the faithful and wise servant in Matthew 24:42-51, Jesus indicated that He would come back, and that we should not lose hope of that coming — even if He tarries a long time. He said: *"Blessed is that servant, whom his lord when he cometh shall find him so doing"* (vs. 46). Jesus continues: *"But . . . if that evil servant shall say in his heart, My lord delayeth his coming; And shall begin to smite his fellowservants, and to eat and drink with the drunken; The lord of that servant shall come in a day when he looketh not for him, and in an hour that he is not aware of"* (vss. 48-50).

Rather than be like such an unprofitable servant, Jesus indicated that we should "occupy" until He comes as shown in Luke 19:13. This means we should be on the job when He returns, no matter when that is. So, let us not grow weary if He tarries a while longer.

For, even if He should delay His coming for another hundred years or more, someday He *will* come for each of us, and we will need to be ready when His call comes for us. Truly, though, I believe His coming will not be delayed much longer.

4. *Hold to the world very loosely*. It is easy for Christians to become entangled with the world until the spiritual side of life goes begging. Jesus instructs us: "*. . . take heed to yourselves, lest at any time your hearts be overcharged with surfeiting* [the nauseous after-effects of intoxication] *and drunkenness, and cares of this life* [things which belong to life], *and so that day come upon you unawares*" (Luke 21:34).

   Notice that Jesus puts things belonging to life in the same category as being drunken in their effect of making us unaware of His coming. Sometimes even those things which seem so necessary to life may serve to dull our spiritual sensitivity if not kept in check. I believe it is for this reason that 1 John 2:15 instructs us: "*Love not the world, neither the things which are in the world. . . .*" The danger of loving the world, of course, is that we will become so ensnared in this world that we will forget about the next one.

5. *Cultivate and build our faith*. Jesus said: "*. . . when the Son of man cometh, shall he find faith on the earth?*" (Luke 18:8). These words are more than a rhetorical question. Jesus actually points to a possibility that at the time of His return, faith might be a rare thing on earth! In response to this, it is important to be on the defense against evil. But one vastly

important thing we should do is to engage regularly in activities which will help build and strengthen our faith.

May I suggest five such activities?

1. *Know your Bible!* Evangelical Christians are vitally concerned about truth. When Jesus prayed His high priestly prayer, He indicated that His disciples would be sanctified through the truth. Beyond that, He said: *". . . ye shall know the truth, and the truth shall make you free"* (John 8:32). The Bible contains the truth we need to bc kept in the right way and away from error. Its pages contain the road map to eternal life, as well as instructions for living a fuller and more satisfying Christian life. It contains truth you can get from no other source.

2. *Meditate upon the Bible daily.* The Psalmist said: *"Thy word have I hid in mine heart, that I might not sin against thee"* (Ps. 119:11). Meditating daily upon God's Word helps to keep us strong in the faith by filling our minds with God's will and precepts for our lives.

3. *Pray regularly.* In 1 Thessalonians 5:17, Paul urges us to *". . . Pray without ceasing. . . ."* This means that we should be often in prayer and be continually in the attitude of prayer. It is significant, I think, that this instruction is given to us only a few short sentences before he prays that our whole spirit, soul, and body be preserved blameless unto the coming of our Lord

Jesus Christ (1 Thess. 5:23).

4. *Gather regularly with the church for worship, to hear the Word of God expounded, and to help one another grow in the faith.* There is no real substitute for worshipping with other believers. Listen as the Hebrew writer speaks: *"Let us draw near with a true heart in full assurance of faith. . . . Let us hold fast the profession of our faith without wavering. . . . And let us consider one another to provoke unto love and to good works: Not forsaking the assembling of ourselves together, as the manner of some is; but exhorting one another: and so much the more, as ye see the day approaching"* (Heb. 10:22-25). As you can see, two of the great reasons to gather in worship with the believers is to edify them, and to have yourself edified and built up as well. In addition, you can hear the Word of God preached and explained clearly during the worship services. If that doesn't happen in your church, find one where it does. Join with others in discovering the deep truths of the Bible through preaching, for the Apostle Paul wrote that God chose *". . . the foolishness of preaching to save them that believe"* (1 Cor. 1:21).

5. *Fill your heart and mind with thoughts which build rather than those which tear down.* Philippians 4:8 encourages us to think about those things which are true, honest, pure, lovely, of good report, virtuous, and praiseworthy. Therefore, read edifying literature, watch edifying films, listen to edifying music, think edifying thoughts, form edifying habits. In short, we

should be *". . . bringing into captivity every thought to the obedience of Christ"* (2 Cor. 10:5).

Might I be bold enough to suggest here that if we Christians engage in this kind of activity, it will exclude many kinds of literature, music, and television viewing from our lives? The kinds of things Paul writes about are uplifting and edifying. In contrast, many other kinds of things tear down our faith, spirits, and lives. These activities and habits should be cast aside in favor of those activities and habits which do build us up in the faith.

Allow me to add that certain activities and habits which cannot be considered sinful in the strictest sense, nevertheless, may sometimes need to be forsaken because of slow and almost unseen damage they do to our spiritual state if they are engaged in over an extended period of time. As Paul said in 1 Corinthians 10:23: *"All things are lawful for me, but all things are not expedient: all things are lawful for me, but all things edify not."* And in 1 Corinthians 6:12, he wrote: *". . . all things are lawful for me, but I will not be brought under the power of any."* Let us lay aside whatever weighs us down and engage in those activities and habits which build strong Christian lives.

Let us conclude this first section and turn our attention in another direction. In order to prepare for the last days, we need to be sure we have on the wedding garment, and we need to live in continual readiness for the return of the Master. To do this we need to guard our lifestyles against sinful practices, we need to watch tirelessly for His coming, we need to avoid becoming weary of waiting, we need to hold to this world loosely, and we need to fill our hearts and minds with that which edifies.

But our responsibility does not stop with preparing ourselves. We also have a responsibility to help prepare others. "What should I be doing to prepare others in the last days?" In answer, there are at least four major steps you can take to help prepare others for the coming of the Lord.

1. *Do what you can to spread the gospel.* The job of carrying the gospel to every creature is a large and almost overwhelming task. Fortunately, it is not all yours. The task belongs first and foremost to Jesus who promised, "*. . . and, lo, I am with you always, even unto the end of the world. Amen"* (Matt. 28:20). But your part is as important as the next Christian's part. And if you are not an evangelist, a preacher, or a missionary, you can still be actively involved in world evangelism in a significant way.

   You can do as much as the widow's two mites or planting a mustard seed. You can befriend that unsaved person in your neighborhood and share the gospel with him. While what you do may not seem very significant, never underestimate the value of your own work in the kingdom of God. As the song writer has said: "Little is much if God is in it."

2. *Learn how to actively lead others to Christ.* I can

almost hear someone saying even now: "Oh, no, here comes the rap we get from the pulpit every Sunday about 'every Christian an evangelist.' " But, if that is your expectation, I am going to disappoint you. Not every Christian is an evangelist in the sense that not every Christian has been given the spiritual gift of evangelism. But, every Christian can and does play a part in the salvation of others in the world; for, even though we are not all evangelists, every Christian will have an opportunity to share faith with someone else. It pays to be ready for such occasions with just the right words, the right scriptures, and the right spirit to lead someone else to the Master's care and forgiveness.

3. *Support the Word of God in spiritual and material ways.* There is an old worn triplicate of values for the Christian who desires to help others into the kingdom of God. Though worn from much use, it is still valuable. It is this — pray, give, and go. The work of God still needs people who can intercede for the lost. He still needs people who can and will give to the work of God so that those prayers can be answered. And the work of God still needs those who do the actual work of ministry with the financial assistance and prayer support. As Paul wrote in Romans 10:13-15: *". . . Whosoever shall call upon the name of the Lord shall be saved. How then shall they call on him in whom they have not believed? and how shall they believe in him of whom they have not heard? and how shall they hear without a preacher? And how shall they preach, except they be sent? . . ."*

What has this to do with you? Every Christian can intercede for the lost, worldwide. Many or most Christians can give to support those who are sent with the gospel — whether at home or abroad. And some Christians can and will leave home and family and go with the gospel to other lands. Others will stay at home and continue through many and various means to spread the good news. But every Christian is part of the command of Christ in Matthew 28, to *". . . go into all the world and preach the gospel to every creature."*

Therefore, go if you can. But if you can't go, at least give to support those who are sent. And while you are doing all you can to support the work of God where you can, pray continually for the effectiveness of the gospel everywhere.

This old, worn triplicate of values we've been talking about teaches some great lessons about the nature of the kingdom of God. I suppose one of the greatest is that the kingdom of God must be our highest priority. This leads me to the fourth and final suggestion as to how we can help others prepare for the coming of the Lord.

4. *Make the word of God the number one priority in your life.* Jesus said: *". . . seek ye first the kingdom of God . . ."* (Matt. 6:33). First-place commitment to Christ and to His kingdom may be a more rare commodity among Christians than we would like to think. Perhaps that is so even in our own lives. Let's ask ourselves a few questions: How far up on the priority list of our lives is the work of God? Does the

Lord get first place in the use of our time? Does His work occupy much of our prayer time, or do we spend most of our prayer time asking for ourselves? Does He get first place in the expenditure of our money and the use of our earthly goods? What about our words? Does Christ have first place there? Can He count on us to stand up for Him and tell of His grace in the marketplace of our lives? Or do we hang our heads in fear and shame when someone mentions the fact that we are Christians?

Of all the things clamoring for our allegiance today, the Word of God is the one that offers benefits that are of eternal value. Making the Word of God the first priority in your life will help you help others to prepare for the coming of the Lord.

If we really believe that these are the last days, great responsibility rests upon you and me to be ready ourselves for the great day of the Lord. But this faith also places a great responsibility upon us to help others prepare for that great and terrible day.

Fanny Crosby clearly stated the theme of this message in song. And she asked some very penetrating questions when she wrote:

"When Jesus comes to reward His servants, whether it be noon or night, faithful to Him will He find us watching, with our lamps all trimmed and bright?

"If at the dawn of the early morning He

shall call us one by one, When to the Lord we restore our talents, will He answer thee, well done?

"Blessed are those whom the Lord finds watching; in His glory they shall share. If He comes at the dawn or midnight, will He find us watching there?

"Oh can we say we are ready, Brother, ready for the soul's bright home? Say, will He find you and me still watching, waiting, waiting, when the Lord shall come?"

My friends, if you are not prepared for the Lord's return, please prepare today by accepting Christ as Lord and Savior. And if you are already one of His own, watch and be ready, for He is coming again!